DOBERMAN PINSCHER

CYNTHIA P. GALLAGHER

Doberman Pinscher

Editors: Matthew Haviland,
      Stephanie Fornino
Indexer: Elizabeth Walker
Designer: Angela Stanford
Series Designer: Mary Ann Kahn

TFH Publications®
President/CEO: Glen S. Axelrod
Executive Vice President: Mark E. Johnson
Publisher: Glen S. Axelrod
Associate Publisher: Stephanie Fornino

TFH Publications, Inc.®
One TFH Plaza
Third and Union Avenues
Neptune City, NJ 07753

Discovery Communications, Inc. Book Development Team: Marjorie
Kaplan, President and General Manager, Animal Planet Media/Nicolas
Bonard, GM & SVP, Discovery Studios Group/Robert Marick, VP,
North American Licensing/Sue Perez-Jackson, Director, Licensing/
Tracy Conner, Manager, Licensing

Printed and bound in China

16 17 18 19 20 21   1 3 5 7 9 8 6 4 2

Library of Congress Cataloging-in-Publication Data
Names: Gallagher, Cynthia P., author.
Title: Doberman pinscher / Cynthia P. Gallagher.
Description: Neptune City, NJ : T.F.H. Publications, Inc., [2016] | Series:
  Animal planet. Dogs 101 | Includes bibliographical references and index.
Identifiers: LCCN 2015036492 | ISBN 9780793837403 (hardcover : alk. paper)
Subjects: LCSH: Doberman pinscher.
Classification: LCC SF429.D6 G35 2016 | DDC 636.73/6--dc23
LC record available at http://lccn.loc.gov/2015036492

This book has been published with the intent to provide accurate and authoritative information in regard to the
subject matter within. While every reasonable precaution has been taken in preparation of this book. the author
and publisher expressly disclaim responsibility for any errors, omissions, or adverse effects arising from the use
or application of the information contained herein. The techniques and suggestions are used at the reader's
discretion and are not to be considered a substitute for veterinary care. If you suspect a medical problem consult
your veterinarian.

Note: In the interest of concise writing, "he" is used when referring to puppies and dogs unless the text is
specifically referring to females or males. "She" is used when referring to people. However, the information
contained herein is equally applicable to both sexes.

The Leader In Responsible Animal Care for Over 50 Years!®
www.tfh.com

CONTENTS

ORIGINS OF YOUR
DOBERMAN PINSCHER

"The greatest love is a mother's, then a dog's, then a sweetheart's." Any dog lover will concur with this Polish proverb, but perhaps none so heartily as the Doberman Pinscher's. Those who have been lucky enough to belong to a Doberman know firsthand the breed's loyalty, intelligence, and affectionate nature, not to mention elegant and impressive appearance.

But the Doberman Pinscher, or Dobie, is among several breeds that languish under misconceptions about their perceived "vicious" natures. Like the bully breeds (the American Pit Bull Terrier, the Staffordshire Bull Terrier, etc.) and the Rottweiler, Dobies have been mistaken for aggressive dogs who are eminently suitable for guarding and law enforcement but unsafe as family companions. Although we will see that the Doberman's origins indeed lie in protection, this admirable breed has evolved into a fun-loving, affectionate, and enjoyable pet.

THE DEVELOPMENT OF THE DOG

The roots of our beautiful friendship with dogs are set deeply in human history. Cave drawings of bison, cattle, and wolves depict prehistoric man's relationship with animals and foreshadow the bond we would have with pets. For a long time, scholars believed that dogs descended from gray wolves, but some now claim that they are not as closely related as previously thought.

Modern research suggests that both dogs and gray wolves descended from an earlier canid ancestor as far back as 100,000 years ago. Geographically speaking, some experts say early dogs originated in the Middle East, while others maintain that they came from eastern Asia. Still others believe their origins lie in central Europe.

How did mankind domesticate early dog? Some studies proffer that ancient wolf-dogs assisted human hunter-gatherers in bringing down large prey, thus beginning their symbiotic relationship and early dog's domestication. Given that dogs have retained their ancestral pack-animal instincts, people may have assumed the dominant role in the pack. As early dogs learned obedience, tamer ones would have been inclined to remain with this new kind of pack leader. Natural selection then likely produced tamer and tamer dogs until the domestic dog eventually evolved.

No one can say for certain how man and dog became such fast friends, but we do know that the earliest dogs assisted man in hunting. Their descendents also helped people in battle, farming, and other pursuits, all the way to the present day. Now they are indispensible to us, not only as companions but also in their capacities as service workers, therapy dogs, and search-and-rescue dogs, for which the Doberman Pinscher is especially suited.

HISTORY OF THE DOBERMAN PINSCHER

The Dobie we know today is actually a relative newcomer to the purebred-dog world. Developed in the late 19th century, the sleek and powerful companion we now call the Doberman Pinscher was produced through combining several different breeds.

The Doberman's stereotype as a guard dog is rooted in fact and purpose. In the late 1800s, a German tax collector named Karl Friedrich Louis Dobermann from Apolda, Thuringia, endeavored to develop a superior guardian breed to protect him on collection rounds. Dissatisfied with the breeds available to him, Herr Dobermann envisioned a protector large enough to intimidate potential robbers yet not too large to handle and care for easily. He wanted an intelligent dog who was readily trainable with a short coat that required minimal grooming. He wanted an alert, protective dog who would be aggressive when the situation called for it.

Fortunately for Herr Dobermann, his job as a night watchman for the Public Dog Shelter of Apolda afforded him access to many types of breeds with which he could dabble. The eclectic Dobermann was also a dogcatcher, which gave him access to many stray dogs. By 1880, he was deeply immersed in creating his ideal breed.

Dogs share common ancestry with wolves, but their origins have been debated.

BREEDING THE DOBERMAN PINSCHER

Unfortunately for history, Herr Dobermann was not the best record keeper. Although he meticulously chose the breeds that contributed to the dog who would ultimately bear his name, he failed to carefully record his breedings. Thus we cannot truly know the exact lineage of the Doberman Pinscher, nor in what proportions various breeds contributed their individual traits.

Historians have identified several breeds either known to or that appear to have been used in the development of Dobermann's dream dog. The German Pinscher had the terrier qualities of alertness, tenacity, and aggressiveness that Dobermann sought; the Beauceron provided size, substance, intelligence, and a desire to please; the Manchester Terrier contributed the short, shiny coat and elegant appearance; the Weimaraner (known then as the Weimar Pointer) also had the easy-care short coat, along with scenting abilities and retrieving skills; and the Rottweiler provided size, stamina, intelligence, and working abilities.

Multiple breeds mentioned above provided coloration, and a German sheepdog called the Thuringian Shepherd (a now-extinct breed associated with the German Shepherd Dog we know today) may have contributed physicality and a strong work ethic to the mix. Some histories also mention Great Danes, German Shorthaired Pointers, and other breeds in the Doberman Pinscher's ancestry, though we will never know for sure.

Passing the Torch

Herr Dobermann's health began to fail in the latter part of the century, after more than a decade of breeding. Unwilling to let his work wither on the vine, he passed his vision to Otto Göller, owner of the von Thüringen Kennel. Upon Dobermann's death in 1894, it fell to Göller to promote interest in the breed Dobermann had so carefully created and to continue improving it. It was around this time that some historians say Göller added Greyhounds to the "recipe" for added height and speed, while others maintain that this actually occurred during Dobermann's work. Without written records, it is impossible to know which breeds went into the mix at what time.

What we do know is that Dobermann and Göller achieved the former's goal in developing an effective working dog with strong protective instincts. The early Dobermans were more heavyset and had larger heads than today's Dobies. They more closely resembled Rottweilers than modern Doberman Pinschers, with somewhat coarse coats that tended to be wavy and of short to medium length.

Completing the Breed

Some core Doberman Pinschers produced around 1896 are considered the breed's founding ancestors. These eight dogs were of the heavier-set, longer-haired early type, but several of their desirable traits were perpetuated.

Remember that Dobermans were developed with a specific purpose in mind. Characteristics such as courage and aggressiveness were more important than appearance. One of the core dogs in particular, Lux, was known to have a very aggressive nature. This core group spawned Dobermans who soon earned the breed the fearsome reputation that has persisted to this day.

Several breeds contributed to the Doberman Pinscher's strength, intelligence, and protective nature.

Temperament notwithstanding, appearance also continued to be honed, and with valid reason. Adequate size was needed for strength and substance, but a lean physique would provide agility and athleticism. Notable refinements to the early Doberman's appearance were made by another Herr Dobermann successor, Goswin Tischler, who was instrumental in developing the sleek, elegant dog we know today. The owner of Apolda's von Grönland Kennel, Tischler also produced the first champion Doberman, Prinz Matzi von Grönland, and was credited with producing the famous "five-star litter," the five exceptional offspring of Lux and Tilly I (two core Dobermans).

Other physical changes were also introduced, though these have since become controversial. A fierce, intimidating mien was achieved by cropping the floppy ears into upstanding points, and at some point during early breed development, some pups were born with bobbed tails, a mutation that became popular. This may be why the modern Doberman's long tail is traditionally docked after birth. Both ear cropping and tail docking are now restricted in many countries.

Not only the breed but also its name evolved during the late 1800s. Early on, Dobermans were called Dobermann's Dogs and Thüringen Pinschers. When these aggressive, fearless guardians began working with law enforcement and the military, they were called *Soldatenhunds* (Soldier Dogs). Eventually, their official name became Dobermannpinscher, which followed the German style of merging words in compound nouns. While the American name would be Doberman Pinscher (two words, without the second *n*), the European name would later become simply Dobermann.

THE 20TH-CENTURY DOBERMAN

The early 20th century proved a difficult time in Doberman Pinscher history. World War I devastated much of Europe with food shortages and starvation, and many dogs were put to death because people were unable to feed or care for them. This became devastating to Doberman breeding kennels. Prominent breeder Philipp Gruenig recounts in *The Dobermann Pinscher: History and Development of the Breed* that many of his kennel's Dobermans died during the war. Eighteen of his puppies were euthanized; two prized dogs died of malnutrition soon after.

To save their breeding stock from the ravages of war, many German breeders exported their Dobermans. Additionally, the German government needed Dobermans for military and police service. These two factors saved the newly developed breed from severe compromise. Many of Germany's foremost breeding Dobermans ended up in foreign countries, including the United States. This not only salvaged the breed but also spread Doberman Pinscher awareness throughout the world.

By the time, the Doberman's numbers in post–World War I Germany began to recover, their stability was once again threatened, this time by World War II.

Doberman Pinschers
were exported to
preserve Germany's
breeding stock during
World War I.

Doberman Pinschers were exported to preserve Germany's breeding stock during World War I.

The Nazi Party controlled all dog breeding and exportation, putting most of the country's Dobermans to use in the military and severely restricting their exportation abroad. German Shepherd Dogs and Doberman Pinschers are often seen at the side of SS officers in historical photographs of concentration camps, a role in the breed's history that most fanciers would rather forget.

Fortunately, the Doberman's longevity was boosted by America's use of military service dogs during the war. The Marine Corps's dog of choice? The Doberman Pinscher. With help from the Doberman Pinscher Club of America (DPCA) and the Dogs for Defense recruiting program, the Marines recruited numerous Dobermans for military service. Many DPCA members screened military-dog candidates, donating their resources to help find the best recruits available.

Dobermans continued their admirable service during the Korean and Vietnam wars, but their loyalty and valor during World War II made them legendary. Many years later, Dr. William Putney, a veterinarian who served with the Marines during World War II, wanted to pay homage to the dogs who saved his and countless other lives in Guam. He campaigned to replace Guam's overgrown war-dog cemetery with a monument honoring those fallen dogs. That monument was unveiled in 1994 at Naval Base Guam. A life-sized statue of Kurt, a Doberman who served with distinction, lies guard atop the memorial, which bears an inscription of the US Marine Corps's motto, *Semper Fidelis* (Always Faithful).

THE DOBERMAN PINSCHER IN AMERICA

The Doberman Pinscher was first imported into the United States in 1908. That same year, a male named Doberman Intelectus, bred by Doberman Kennels in Pittsford, New York, became the first Doberman registered with the American Kennel Club (AKC). It wouldn't be until 1939 that the breed won Best in Show at the famed Westminster Kennel Club Dog Show. That year's winner, Ch. Ferry v. Rauhfelsen of Giralda, would go on to produce 17 American champions.

The Doberman Pinscher Club of America was officially founded in 1921 by George Howard Earle III, who would become governor of Pennsylvania and serve in World War II as President Franklin D. Roosevelt's special emissary to the Balkans. The DPCA adopted the Doberman Pinscher's German breed standard in 1922 but replaced it with an AKC-approved American standard in 1935.

Ongoing efforts to soften the Doberman's temperament and public image have steadily improved his popularity.

The breed soon experienced an increase in popularity. By 1934, the AKC had more than 1,000 Doberman registrations each year. But their reputation for aggression became popular opinion, and Doberman Pinschers were viewed by the public as loose cannons who could "turn on their masters" at any time. This fear ran so deep that the 1939 Westminster Best-in-Show winner is said to have won the competition without the judge ever physically examining him!

The Doberman's reputation wasn't entirely unfounded. After all, Herr Dobermann set out to develop a protective guardian, so little wonder that the American public was wary of this handsome breed. Of course, Dobermans would soon be favored by the Nazis as military guard dogs. To make matters worse, some veteran dogs from the Korean War and World War II were rehomed without benefit of rehabilitation to civilian life. These dogs had difficulty adjusting, often exhibiting behavioral problems, much like human veterans experiencing post-traumatic stress disorder (PTSD).

By the 1960s, highly publicized incidences of Dobermans attacking, (and in a few cases, even killing) small children fueled the media fire that rendered the breed "dangerous." As with Rottweilers and the bully breeds, who suffered from generalized reputations for aggression, Dobermans involved in cases of aggression were summarily blamed, without full disclosure of the details leading up to the attacks.

The media perpetuated the Doberman's unsavory reputation throughout the 1970s with a string of films portraying the breed as the perennial bad guy. Even as recently as 2009, the Disney-Pixar film *Up* portrayed a Doberman as the leader of a gang of bad dogs.

But thanks to ongoing efforts to soften the Doberman Pinscher's temperament and public image, the breed's popularity has steadily climbed. Celebrity owners like President John F. Kennedy, William Shatner, and Mariah Carey have reinforced the message that Dobermans have star quality as family companions. So if you're up to the challenge of training and exercising a Dobie, you'll find yourself with a loyal family member whose love for you may be only slightly less than your mother's.

CHARACTERISTICS OF YOUR DOBERMAN PINSCHER

No matter which breed you prefer, it's hard to deny the elegant beauty of the Doberman Pinscher. With his striking good looks, ever-alert demeanor, and modest grooming needs, he has earned a worldwide popularity that is well deserved. As we all know, however, looks aren't everything. When searching for a lifetime companion, personality and temperament are important considerations. If you're thinking of adding a Dobie to the family, consider the big picture. The powerful presence and athleticism some consider desirable may prove a concern for others.

But it's imperative to discern truth from hype, so don't let urban legends guide your decision. Do the research. Evaluate your needs and desires in a pet. Weigh these against the physical and emotional needs of a Doberman. If everything lines up, you and the Doberman Pinscher just might be made for each other.

PHYSICAL CHARACTERISTICS

Despite his larger-than-life presence, the Doberman is actually a medium-sized dog, the result of deliberate planning on the part of breed founder Karl Friedrich Louis Dobermann. As with any breed in the American Kennel Club's (AKC) Working Group, the Dobie's size enables him to get his job done effectively. But he is not so large that he is cumbersome to have around or difficult to care for.

GENERAL APPEARANCE

The Dobie's overall presence is impressive. His sleek but powerful physique is equal to tasks that require strength, speed, or agility. His lean frame and high-tucked belly hearken back to the Greyhound ancestry believed to have been added late in his breed development. He has the well-sprung ribs and strong, wide loins of a working dog. He carries himself proudly, as if he is fully aware of his noble origins and wants everyone else to appreciate them, too!

Dobermans are powerful working dogs who carry themselves proudly.

Doberman Pinschers convey enormous power for medium-sized dogs.

SIZE

Male Dobermans usually weigh between 85 and 95 pounds (38.5 and 43 kg), while females weigh between 70 and 80 pounds (32 and 36.5 kg). Because of the breed's muscularity, the typical Dobie's weight belies his stature. Males stand between 26 and 28 inches (66 and 71 cm) tall at the shoulders, while females are slightly smaller at 24 to 26 inches (61 to 66 cm).

Notwithstanding variations for gender, the Doberman Pinscher comes in only one size. Some people mistake the Miniature Pinscher, a toy breed that resembles the Doberman, for a smaller version. In fact, it is an entirely different breed belonging to an entirely different breed group. If you're looking for a pocket-sized Doberman, don't confuse the two!

HEAD AND EYES

The Dobie's regal head complements his sleek body. His triangular skull widens from a long nose to the base of the ears, forming a wedge shape discernable from the top as well as the side. Eyes are close-set due to the slight stop (the drop from the eyes to the bridge of the nose). They are almond-shaped and preferably dark in color. Eye shades will vary with coat color, but the general rule of thumb is the darker, the better. Contrary to myth, a narrow forehead does not indicate a lack of intelligence; the Dobie is one of the world's most intelligent dog breeds.

EARS

When left uncropped, the Dobie's ears have a slight rise to their base, rather than lying close down like a Beagle's or Basset Hound's. When correctly cropped, they stand erect in sharp projections that represent Herr Dobermann's vision of the ideal guard dog: keenly alert and properly imposing.

Ear cropping is a subject of much controversy. The AKC prefers cropped ears in the show ring but exhibits understanding for the growing numbers of dog aficionados who see no merit or purpose in ear cropping. Ironically, the Doberman Pinscher originated in a country that today outlaws the practice of cosmetic ear cropping.

To crop or not is a matter of choice in the United States. If you're unsure about cropping, consider the look you wish your Dobie to present. Cropped ears are attractive on the Dobie's wedge-shaped head, while uncropped ears are gentle and floppy, giving the dog a much tamer appearance.

Remember, ear cropping is a surgical procedure that carries some inherent risk and must be performed while puppies are still young, so carefully weigh the pros

Healthy Doberman Pinschers should have sleek, shiny coats.

and cons before making your decision. There is no scientific proof that cropped ears run less risk of ear infection, so be sure to differentiate fact from fiction when considering the issue.

TAIL

The AKC breed standard specifies docking tails at approximately the second joint. According to the standard, the bobbed tail "appears to be a continuation of the spine." Veterinarians typically dock tails when puppies are just a day or two old. Some say the procedure is long forgotten by the time the wounds are healed. Most breeders will have their puppies' tails docked soon after birth, so you won't have much say in the matter.

Docking is only a requirement for conformation showing, so if you do have an opportunity to decide whether to dock your Dobie's tail, it's up to you whether or not he will have a "distinctive" look. As with ear cropping, tail docking has been a subject of controversy. The American Veterinary Medical Association (AVMA) has recommended removing both from breed standards.

COLORS

The Doberman Pinscher is often identified by his black coat with rust markings, but the AKC breed standard allows for several color variations: black, red, blue (gray), and fawn (a tan shade also known as Isabella). All colors are usually accented with rust-colored markings on the legs and feet, above each eye, below the tail, and on the muzzle, throat, and chest. The AKC does allow for the occasional white patch on the chest, as long as it doesn't exceed .5 square inches (1.5 sq cm). Nose colors should correspond with coat colors, as follows:

COAT	NOSE
black	black
red	dark brown
blue	dark gray
fawn (Isabella)	dark tan

No matter the color, the coat is short and lies close to the body. A healthy, properly groomed Dobie's coat is shiny and sleek, enhancing the breed's graceful body. The hair is straight and flat, without any perceptible waves or ridges. One look and there can be no question that the Doberman Pinscher is one of the handsomest breeds around.

LIVING WITH THE DOBERMAN PINSCHER

The Doberman Pinscher was initially developed as a stocky, aggressive dog who suited Herr Dobermann's purposes as a protector. Today he is an elegant, athletic, intelligent companion prized for his loyalty to family. Still, the Doberman Pinscher is not a breed for everyone. Like all breeds, he has inherent physical and emotional needs that a qualified owner should be prepared to meet.

PERSONALITY

Working dogs like having a job to do, and while the Doberman Pinscher still considers protection his duty, the breed standard specifically states that his temperament should not be vicious. Likewise, he should not present excessive shyness. Today's Dobie should be willing to protect his home and family using sound judgment, not knee-jerk reactions.

Even so, the Doberman Pinscher is not always receptive to strangers, even friendly strangers. His independent nature means he has a mind of his own when it comes to selecting friends. A Dobie will size up a person's intentions before accepting her as a friend, so the casual encounter during a walk may not be enough to motivate your Dobie to warmly greet a stranger. This is something to consider if you want him to be the neighborhood social butterfly. On the other hand, there's no better breed to have around if you worry about home invasions or suspicious strangers.

COMPANIONABILITY

The bottom line is that the Doberman Pinscher's discriminating preferences mean that when he likes someone, he *really* likes her. His strongest attachment will be to the person who cares for and trains him, making him a steadfast companion. His intelligence requires a good deal of human interaction, so if you're not ready to have a pet who wants to be with you as much as possible, the

PUPPY POINTER

Before you bring a puppy into your home, decide with your family what the rules will be regarding your new family member. Encourage everyone to stick to these rules. If you don't want your new Dobie on the furniture, for example, don't allow him on the couch, even when those cute puppy-dog eyes plead with you. Hit-or-miss attempts to honor household rules will confuse him and encourage behavior that will be harder to change later on. Consistency is the key to teaching a new puppy the household routine.

Doberman Pinscher may not be the best breed for you. But after all, isn't loving companionship the reason most of us want a pet in the first place?

With Children

The unenlightened may think that because he was developed for protection and intimidation, the Doberman Pinscher is not a logical choice for a family with children. Experienced Dobie owners will tell you that the breed is generally very good with children and makes an excellent family dog.

Austin H. of Severna Park, Maryland, said that his Dobie, Junior, and his 14-year-old son, Zach, are really like brothers. "Junior would prefer to sleep with Zach," said Austin, "and likes to go wherever he goes. . . . To watch the two of them play, you would scratch your head, wondering which one was the boy and which one was the dog."

As with any dog of any breed, early socialization is the key to establishing acceptance of anything or anyone new. What is the proper way to introduce your dog and your children? It depends on who was in the household first. When bringing a new baby or child home to a family with a dog and no other children, you should acclimate your dog beforehand. Hopefully your dog was socialized to children as a puppy and is responsive to you in obeying basic commands. This earlier experience will help with getting him ready for your incoming family member.

- Prepare your Doberman for the new arrival by handling him more like a child would, focusing on the ears, tail, and paws. Start by petting him and progress to gentle pulling, just as a toddler might. When your dog passively accepts this kind of contact, reward him with praise and treats. Ask some young relatives or neighborhood kids to interact with him, praising and treating him for good behavior during these interactions.
- Teach your dog not to snatch food or toys away from your hand but to take them gently when instructed to do so (many people use the command *easy* or *gently*). Consult your breeder or a qualified trainer for training advice. Once he's mastered this command, practice with the help of kids. This will teach your dog not to steal food or toys from young children, as a jealous older sibling is often tempted to do!
- Modify your routine in anticipation of the new arrival. If your dog is used to spending all his time with you, gradually reduce the amount of time you spend together so that there is no abrupt change to his schedule when the child arrives.
- After your new baby is delivered but before she's brought home, have Dad bring home a hospital blanket or bunting with her scent on it. Present it to your dog so that he can acquaint himself with the scent of the newcomer. Your baby then won't be so much of a stranger to your dog when she does come home.
- Teach your dog to associate the new family member with pleasurable things. When your child comes home, reward your dog with praise and a treat when they are together. Don't be tempted to put your Doberman away in a different room or reprimand him harshly when the child's around. He'll only come to believe that this new arrival has changed his life for the worse.

Dog Tale

Silent-film star Rudolph Valentino had such a strong bond with his Doberman Pinscher, Kabar, that he brought him everywhere, in first class—no shipboard kennels for this dog! No one knows why Valentino chose not to take Kabar to New York during the summer of 1926. When Valentino died that summer from perforated ulcers, peritonitis, and pleurisy, Kabar was heard howling at his Beverly Hills estate. According to the Doberman's 1929 *Chicago Sunday Tribune* obituary, Kabar was "almost constantly sick" in the years that followed.

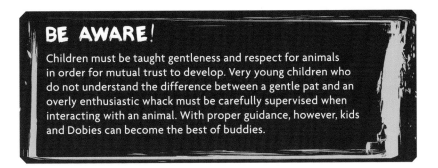

BE AWARE!

Children must be taught gentleness and respect for animals in order for mutual trust to develop. Very young children who do not understand the difference between a gentle pat and an overly enthusiastic whack must be carefully supervised when interacting with an animal. With proper guidance, however, kids and Dobies can become the best of buddies.

When bringing a new dog into a household with children, socialization must be mutual. While a Doberman puppy raised with proper supervision and respect will become devoted to all family members, make sure your kids understand socialization and the appropriate ways to interact with a puppy. They need to realize that pets aren't toys and must be handled gently.

It's never a good idea to bring a puppy into a household with children too young to understand how to properly behave around him. The risk of accidental injury to toddlers from sharp puppy teeth and pointy toenails is too great, as is that of their unintentionally frightening or hurting him. Best to wait until children are old enough to understand the responsibility involved in adding a puppy to the family.

Adult Dobies may not be as enthusiastic as puppies and should be properly introduced and socialized into the environment to overcome any hesitancy or aloofness. If the dog is older, make sure he is comfortable around your children before committing to adopting him. Some older dogs who aren't accustomed to children may not take kindly to them, especially when food or toys are involved.

When they are old enough, children should be encouraged to participate in training and other activities surrounding the new dog. This not only teaches your children responsibility but teaches your dog that children are higher in the social hierarchy than he is. Most importantly, always make sure child(ren) and dog are supervised by an adult.

With Other Pets

How well your dog gets along with other pets has less to do with the breed and more to do with genetics and life experience. Dobies are generally good with other family pets as long as they are introduced properly and have positive experiences. Here again, socialization at an early age is the best way to develop positive experiences with other animals.

A high-energy Doberman Pinscher may be annoying to established pets much the same way a pesky little brother or sister annoys their older siblings. Proper socialization and sufficient exercise should take care of this issue. It's important to show respect to established pets, too, which means removing a particularly persistent puppy from another pet who is just not in the mood to be bothered.

With Other Dogs

A Dobie in a multi-dog household will become part of the social order dogs naturally establish among themselves. Dominant personalities can clash, and it has nothing to do with aggression or intolerance. Males and females in a pack typically establish who holds the alpha positions, and pets are no different. For this reason, conventional wisdom says to avoid, when possible, adding another male dog to an already established male pet. Likewise with females. This is not to say that multiple dogs of the same sex can't and won't coexist harmoniously, but it's best to mix genders when possible.

Two dogs should meet on neutral turf to avoid territorial behavior. Both should be leashed but allowed to sniff and circle each other in the age-old manner of

Dobies are generally good around other pets when given proper introductions and positive shared experiences.

When choosing your Doberman puppy from a litter, evaluate every dog for health and temperament before making your decision. Reputable breeders should be able to guarantee (in writing) the health of their puppies, something you may not receive from hobby breeders or Internet ads.

As for temperament, examine each puppy when you meet them. Don't make the mistake of thinking that the most outgoing, boldest puppy will make the best family pet. An exceptionally dominant Doberman pup can prove difficult to train. Nor should you fall for the cuteness appeal of "runts." Very shy dogs with low confidence may develop trust issues, especially toward strangers, and fear biting may result. Temperament extremes in Dobermans can cause problems that are more serious than for other dog breeds.

canine greeting. Most adult dogs are tolerant of puppies, but keep a weather eye on both in case any resentment on the part of the established dog should manifest. Don't leave an established family dog alone with a new puppy until you're confident in their compatibility. Even then, an adult dog may get too rough in play, so it's best to be chaperone. As time goes by, a natural hierarchy between the two should emerge.

With Cats and Small Pets

Introducing your Doberman (or any breed) to an established family cat requires diplomacy. If you are adopting your Dobie from a shelter or rescue organization, they should be able to tell you if he has been cat-socialized. Cats usually resent intruders either way and will keep their distance for a few weeks until reconciled that the new addition is there to stay.

When introducing your new Doberman and your cat for the first time, defer to the cat's rank. If your new Dobie is a puppy, hold him and let the cat sniff around him freely. If he is older or an adult, put him in a crate and let the cat sniff him out. Never leave them alone unsupervised until you are sure of their compatibility.

Smaller pets, like rodents, should be kept away from dogs and cats, who are their natural predators. It's nice to envision a peaceable kingdom in your home, but it's not realistic. We've all seen the endearing Internet videos of a pet bird sitting on top of a pet cat's head, but that's the exception, not the norm.

ENVIRONMENT

Dobies are versatile dogs who can adapt to different living situations, making them as comfortable in an apartment as on a large farm. As long as they get plenty of exercise, they are flexible enough to be comfortable almost anywhere. Of course, common sense plays a role here. If you live in an apartment so tiny that there is barely room for you, it's not a good idea to get a dog the size of a Doberman Pinscher. If your house doesn't have room for a crate, dog beds, and a peaceful nook for your Dobie to eat his meals and access water, consider a smaller breed.

Similarly, if you envision a pet who happily lives in a doghouse out back, the Doberman may not be for you. Dogs generally should not be kept outside, and Dobermans are especially unfit for this lifestyle. Their athletic prowess and protective instincts might convey the impression that they would make good "outside" dogs, but there are two reasons that refute this.

One, they don't like to be left alone for long periods of time. Dobies are happiest being with the family, preferably beside you on the couch. Even living indoors, if they must be alone all day while the family is at school and work, they may develop behavioral or emotional issues. Dogs are social animals who don't like isolation, and this is especially true of Dobermans.

Two, the Dobie's short, close-lying coat makes him especially vulnerable to cold temperatures. He lacks the protective undercoat that makes many breeds more weather tolerant, so he needs to live comfortably indoors with his humans. Even in warm weather, biting insects and external parasites can make his life miserable, so let your Dobie share your home as well as your affections.

EXERCISE REQUIREMENTS

The Doberman Pinscher is a member of the AKC's Working Group, which means he has the desire and the physicality to lead an active lifestyle. Intelligent dogs like the Doberman Pinscher thrive with activities to do and jobs to perform. Sufficient exercise stimulates them mentally and keeps their bodies healthy and toned.

One look at the Doberman Pinscher tells you that he wants and needs a lot of activity. Just because he enjoys cuddling on the couch doesn't mean he's content to spend all his time there. A committed Dobie owner will spend about half an hour twice a day in vigorous aerobic exercise with her dog, whether that means brisk, long walks, rousing games of fetch, or jogging or cycling. Dobies are excellent candidates for organized dog sports such as flyball, agility, and Schutzhund. No matter what activity you choose, your

Dobermans thrive with activities to do and jobs to perform.

Dobie will enjoy the quality time spent with you as much as he does the activity itself.

Observe your Dobie for signals of exhaustion. When he gets tired, slow down. On warm days, provide plenty of water during exercise. Although puppies seem to have boundless energy, they also tire out eventually. When introducing two- to four-month-old pups to leash walking, keep the walks to about five minutes at a time. Limit play periods, too—no more than ten minutes or so. As puppies grow, their exercise and play periods can be extended accordingly.

TRAINABILITY

Not only does the Dobie's intelligence make him a very trainable breed, but it also makes training a must. Working dogs were bred to perform jobs; they need to be occupied mentally as well as physically. A bored dog can become a destructive, unhappy dog who gets into trouble.

Training should begin early in your Doberman's life and continue throughout his life. Some dogs have more tenacious and precocious personalities than their littermates, boldly going where other dogs fear to tread. It's important that dogs who push the limits understand that they must learn the boundaries as well.

SUPPLIES FOR YOUR
DOBERMAN PINSCHER

Dog beds should be big enough for your Doberman's adult size.

Responsible dog ownership involves preparation. After all, you wouldn't bring home your newborn baby without having first stocked up on diapers, bathing supplies, bottles, et cetera, right? Having the right supplies for your new Doberman Pinscher is just as important. This doesn't mean you need to spend a fortune at your local pet-supply store, but laying in a few essentials will go a long way toward a smooth transition for your Doberman Pinscher into his new family.

BEDS

Every dog needs a cozy place to lay his head, so a comfortable pet bed should be one of your first purchases. The Doberman Pinscher likes to be near his people, so it's not unreasonable to scatter a few beds through the house in rooms where the family spends most of its time. Keep in mind that a dog can relax as happily on nothing more than a pillow or a couple of blankets as he can on a memory-foam bolster bed.

Whichever dog bed you prefer, it should be large enough to accommodate an adult Dobie (puppy-sized beds will need to be replaced several times before your Dobie is full-grown) and thick enough to support a Doberman's frame without his elbows rubbing on a hard surface. Opt for a washable bed, or at least one with washable covers. Even with the cleanest of dogs, dog beds can quickly become dirty and smelly from body oils and dander, so washable bedding is a must.

Avoid dog beds featuring buttons, tassels, or other decorations that could be chewed or torn off and turn into a choking hazard. Nor should you choose a bed with a wicker frame. Wicker poses too great a chewing temptation for puppies (who will chew anything they can get their jaws on) and for adults who might be bored or stressed. When it comes to safe, comfortable beds for your Dobie, less is often more.

COLLARS

Your Dobie will need to wear a collar at some point in his life, even if he goes without one inside the house. Collars come in various materials, such as nylon, leather, and metal, and they fasten with snap-in or belt-type buckles or clasps. Get something adjustable, comfortable, and secure.

Not all collars are created equal. Chain (or "choke-chain") collars come with a ring on either end and form a loop around the dog's neck, tightening and loosening as he pulls on the leash. These can hurt your dog's trachea, cause difficulty breathing, and promote stress and discomfort. As such, they should never be used (whether for training, regular walking, or otherwise).

Whichever type of adjustable collar you choose, make sure it's the right size for your Dobie as he grows. A properly fitting collar should rotate easily around his neck but not be so loose that he can wriggle out of it. A good test of fit is if you can easily place two fingers between the collar and his neck.

Make sure your Doberman's collar is the right size for him as he grows.

Most collars come with a metal D-ring where you can attach the all-important ID tag containing contact information in case your dog ever becomes lost. Many manufacturers offer the option of stitching a name and

PUPPY POINTER

Puppies will take some time to get used to wearing a collar. At first they will scratch at this strange new accessory and attempt to get it off, but they will soon get used to it as long as it's comfortable to wear.

phone number directly into the fabric, which is a foolproof way of ensuring that the collar has identifying information. Tags have been known to be torn off or otherwise become separated from dog collars; information stitched right in will always be there.

Collars with ID information are the fastest, easiest way for a lost dog to be identified. You'll probably want to hang your dog's rabies certification tag on his collar as well. In the event that he becomes lost, it's imperative that anyone who finds him knows that he's been vaccinated.

Many dog owners prefer harnesses, which fasten around your dog's upper body instead of encircling his neck. These alleviate pulling on the neck when walking an energetic Dobie (though proper training on how to walk nicely on leash would also take care of that issue). Whatever collar you choose for your Dobie, be sure it provides him comfort and protection. You'll be glad for the peace of mind.

CRATES

The dog crate is an often-misunderstood piece of equipment. Far from being a prison, it provides a safe haven for the puppy or adult Dobie, his own special refuge. It is also a safe place to restrict your dog if you need him out of the way for a while when you have guests or workmen in the house. If he's been properly crate trained, he won't mind spending some downtime in his own "room," especially if he can still see the goings-on around him. A soft crate cushion and a chew toy or two and he's all set.

Crating your dog has distinct advantages. For one thing, crates are an important tool for potty training. Dogs instinctively want to avoid soiling their bedding, so a puppy will learn to do his business elsewhere (hopefully in an appropriate place) to keep his crate clean and dry. Of course, a puppy can "hold it" only for short periods of time, so don't expect miracles.

Moreover, if you can't take your puppy with you on outings, the crate is the best place for him. Not only will he feel more secure in a cozy nook of his own, but he'll be safe from hazards in the home, like electrical cords and potentially toxic houseplants. Just be sure not to leave him inside for more than an hour (or two at the most). Your puppy's frequent need to potty will set you back in housetraining if he's in the crate so long that he soils it. Plus, his high energy level isn't conducive to long stints being confined. He may become bored, lonely, anxious, or all three. You want him to learn to love his crate, so avoid leaving him in there so long that he regards it as a prison.

CHOOSING A CRATE

Crates come in many different sizes, just as dogs do. To avoid having to upsize the crate as your dog grows, buy one large enough for an adult Dobie and partition off half of it while he is still young and potty training. Without this partition, you will have a crate so large that he can soil one end and still have clean space available in which to relax.

A crate large enough for an adult Dobie takes up space, but it's well worth it to provide him with a room of his own, whether you need to confine him for a few hours or he wants somewhere to get away from the madding crowd and take a nap. Your crate should not be so small that your growing dog will not be able to comfortably sit, stand, and turn around in it when he's an adult.

Crates large enough to accommodate an adult Doberman are often made of thick wire or solid plastic.

Crates are manufactured in various materials, but most that are large enough to accommodate a Doberman Pinscher are made of thick wire or solid plastic. Since the Dobie likes to be with his family, a wire crate that enables him to see everything happening around him is a good choice. Line the bottom with a thick, washable cushion or blanket and you're good to go.

EXERCISE PENS (EX-PENS)

Exercise pens (or "ex-pens") are enclosed pens for puppy play or confinement. They are usually made of flexible wire panels that you can configure to the size you want. They're great for keeping a puppy—or more than one—restricted to a small area, but don't expect them to provide much of a barrier to an adult Dobie. He'll knock them down or simply jump over them! There's another name for ex-pens that are suitable for adults: 6-foot (2.5-m) fences.

FOOD AND WATER BOWLS

Believe it or not, the type of food and water dishes your Dobie uses constitutes an important decision. Commercially manufactured pet bowls for everyday use are typically made from stainless steel, ceramic, or strong plastic, and there are pros and cons to each type that bear consideration.

Plastic bowls are lightweight and unbreakable, but some dogs are allergic to them and may develop skin irritation around the mouth and chin. These bowls may also be made with BPA or other toxic chemicals, which can seep into your dog's food or water. Ceramic bowls can be beautifully decorative and customized with your Dobie's name, but they are subject to breakage and may have toxic glaze or paint. Both plastic and ceramic can develop cracks and crevices that foster bacterial growth.

Stainless steel bowls are your best bet. They may not be works of art, but they are safe to use, easy to clean, and practically indestructible. Look for the kind with rubber rings on the bottom for stabilization.

No matter which bowls you ultimately choose, keep them clean and your dog's water supply fresh and cool. Wash his food dish after every meal

Wash your Doberman's bowls regularly to prevent bacterial growth.

and change his water as often as necessary. Place his bowls where he can enjoy his mealtime undisturbed and have ready access to water at all times.

GATES

Your Dobie may always want to be where you are, but that may not always be safe or convenient. Gated areas are often the best solution when you need to restrict your dog's environment. Gates keep puppies safely within certain areas when you can't maintain a watchful eye on them. They also block off unsafe areas, like steep staircases, for puppies and senior dogs alike.

There are several types of gates available. Some are tension-sprung and can be easily relocated. Others install more permanently by being affixed to the wall with hardware. Whichever type you prefer, look for gates that are sturdy and well made. Beware those with openings in which a puppy can get his head stuck or that he can scale like a rock climber. Also, opt for a gate strong enough to stand up to an adult Dobie who may be a jailbreaker at heart.

GROOMING SUPPLIES

The easy-care Doberman Pinscher doesn't need much grooming to maintain his handsome looks. His short, thin coat requires minimal brushing with a soft-bristle brush to loosen any dirt and help distribute body oils. During the two times a year when he sheds to make room for new growth, a shedding comb can be helpful in removing the loose, dead hair.

Other grooming supplies to keep on hand include nail clippers or a grinding tool for weekly pedicures; cotton balls to keep your dog's ears and eyes clean; dental care supplies; and a bottle of gentle dog shampoo for the occasional bath. We'll discuss grooming in more detail in Chapter 5.

IDENTIFICATION

There is no sadder story than a lost dog with no identification. Even the most vigilant of dog owners cannot predict when her dog will get away from her. Thus, some form of identification for your Dobie is a no-brainer. Even if you just order a collar with your phone number sewn into it, make sure you take steps to provide identifying information on your dog. Don't subject yourself or your Dobie to the stress and potential heartbreak of a lost, unidentified pet.

ID TAGS

ID tags are the most common form of doggy identification. Most pet-supply stores have self-service machines that imprint them in minutes. Tags range from simple circular shapes to brightly colored, blinged-out accessories. Along with the rabies tag your vet provides when your Dobie is inoculated, an ID tag

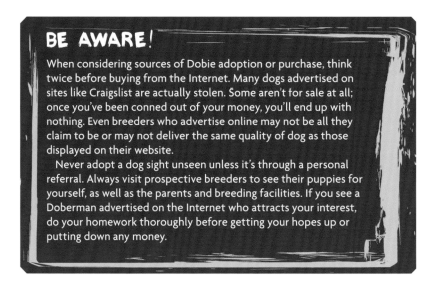

BE AWARE!

When considering sources of Dobie adoption or purchase, think twice before buying from the Internet. Many dogs advertised on sites like Craigslist are actually stolen. Some aren't for sale at all; once you've been conned out of your money, you'll end up with nothing. Even breeders who advertise online may not be all they claim to be or may not deliver the same quality of dog as those displayed on their website.

Never adopt a dog sight unseen unless it's through a personal referral. Always visit prospective breeders to see their puppies for yourself, as well as the parents and breeding facilities. If you see a Doberman advertised on the Internet who attracts your interest, do your homework thoroughly before getting your hopes up or putting down any money.

Dog Tale

Charlie W. of Crownsville, Maryland, knows how smart Dobermans are, especially his own Dobie, Miles. "When Miles was about six months old, I let him off leash to run down the [hiking] trail with me," Charlie said. "He decided to take a detour through the trees. It was a windy evening, and I couldn't hear him running through the leaves. The sun was setting and I started to panic. About ten minutes later, I got in my truck and tried to use the headlights to look for him.

"After no sign of Miles, I parked the truck in the middle of the field [by the trail] and went back into the woods to look for him. I ran the trail and still didn't see him. When I came out, he was sitting next to the passenger side of the truck, waiting for me. After that, I was careful not to let him off leash just before dark. Now when we walk the trail, a lot of the time he'll run off ahead of me and be waiting on the front porch for me to get home and fix his lunch!"

inscribed with your dog's name, your name, and your phone number should be attached to the collar. If the sound of jangling metal annoys you, you can purchase tag silencers: plastic pouches that slip over each one to muffle the noise.

MICROCHIPPING

Microchipping is an effective, inexpensive way to permanently ID your dog. Each microchip carries a unique code read by special scanners and is injected painlessly under your dog's skin. If your dog becomes lost, whoever finds him can bring him to a vet, groomer, or even pet-supply store with a microchip scanner and have him identified. If you register with one of the nationwide microchip registries, they will have your Dobie's code in their database and be able to reunite him with you.

Microchipping is a more reliable way of permanently providing your dog with ID information, as tags and collars can come off. (Database records, of course, will need to be updated if your contact information changes.) It's helpful if your dog is wearing an ID tag with your registry's name and contact information, but there are only a couple of organizations that maintain these databases. Whoever scans the microchip will likely know whom to contact with the scanned ID code.

LEASHES

Given the Doberman Pinscher's powerful build, a strong leash is warranted. Many dog owners prefer the durability and comfort of leather leashes while others prefer flat, woven-nylon leashes, which come in a variety of lengths and colors. Retractable leashes are another option, but these have a thin cord that can be easily snapped by a strong Dobie on a mission. They don't give you reliable control over a breed who warrants more than many due to his size, discriminating preferences (he may warm right up to some people and dogs but stand aloof to others), and reputation. Despite their tempting convenience, you should eschew retractable leashes in favor of a strong, 6-foot (2-m) nylon or leather version.

TOYS

Dobies are not known for being busy dogs, but their intelligence can lead to boredom if they're not active enough. When you can't take yours for regular workouts, you can occupy his mind with puzzle toys. These require him to accomplish a series of tasks in order to obtain a hidden treat. Dogs have

Leather or nylon leashes are your most reliable options.

Few toys beat the good old-fashioned tennis ball with a yard or a dog park.

surprisingly good problem-solving skills, and it's fun to watch them figure out the puzzle for the reward that awaits them.

Dobies have strong jaws, so sturdy chew toys are another important item on your supply list. Not only will they save your shoes, cell phone, or keys from becoming chew toys themselves, but you'll be safeguarding your dog from ingesting something harmful while searching for something else to chew.

Durable artificial chew toys make excellent choices because they don't easily break down into pieces your dog can choke on. They also come in a variety of sizes and flavored coatings. Although rawhide chew toys are popular with dogs and sold ubiquitously, they aren't the best choice. They are known to cause choking, sickness due to contamination, and intestinal blockage. (Dogs will inevitably consume them.)

For a good old-fashioned workout, few toys beat the old-fashioned tennis ball with a large yard or dog park (make sure your dog is properly socialized before visiting the latter). A rousing game of fetch suits the athletic Dobie and doesn't cost a lot. Don't have much of a pitching arm? Pick up one of those inexpensive ball-slingers to do the work for you.

CHAPTER 4

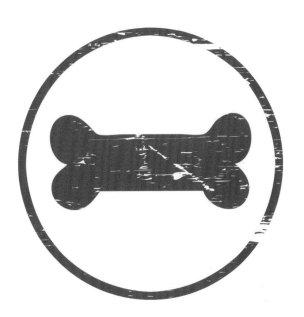

FEEDING YOUR
DOBERMAN PINSCHER

Dogs rarely meet a food they don't like, and just like with kids, they rarely discriminate between what tastes good and what's good for them. After all, when we humans domesticated dogs, it became our responsibility to make sure their nutritional needs were met. In order for your Doberman Pinscher to get the nutrients he needs on a daily basis, you have to familiarize yourself with a few basics.

NUTRITION BASICS

Like with other mammals (including us!), your dog's diet should be composed of carbohydrates, fats, minerals, proteins, vitamins, and water. A diet containing all of these elements is considered complete. It must also be balanced, meaning your Dobie should consume proper amounts of these dietary elements in order for them to work properly together. The following is an overview of each nutrient in your Dobie's healthy diet.

CARBOHYDRATES

Although dogs are primarily carnivorous, they still require carbohydrates in their diet for complete nutrition. Meat doesn't naturally provide the sugars, starches, and cellulose that comprise complex carbohydrates, so your Doberman Pinscher must get them from plant sources: vegetables, whole grains, legumes. Avoid plant foods that the canine anatomy cannot tolerate (such as avocado skin, stems, leaves, and pits) as well as processed carbs that provide only simple starches, like flour and refined rice. About five percent of your Dobie's total diet should come from healthy carbohydrates.

FATS

Fats serve as an energy source and a means of keeping your Dobie's sleek coat looking shiny and healthy. They are also important for healthy skin, eyes, tissue and brain development, and the absorption of fat-soluble vitamins. Plus, they provide essential fatty acids your dog's body doesn't produce on its own.

While they have different nutritional needs, dogs require the same basic nutrients that people do.

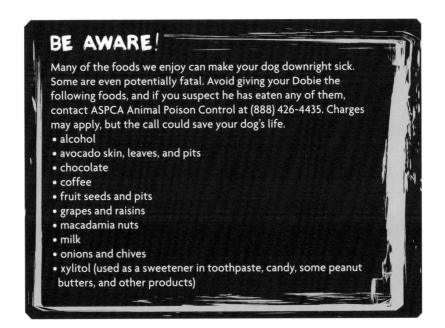

BE AWARE!

Many of the foods we enjoy can make your dog downright sick. Some are even potentially fatal. Avoid giving your Dobie the following foods, and if you suspect he has eaten any of them, contact ASPCA Animal Poison Control at (888) 426-4435. Charges may apply, but the call could save your dog's life.

- alcohol
- avocado skin, leaves, and pits
- chocolate
- coffee
- fruit seeds and pits
- grapes and raisins
- macadamia nuts
- milk
- onions and chives
- xylitol (used as a sweetener in toothpaste, candy, some peanut butters, and other products)

Fats also enhance the taste of food, encouraging good eating habits. Of course, excess fat in your dog's diet will be stored, leading to obesity and its accompanying issues, such as lethargy, joint problems, skin problems, and more. An active Doberman Pinscher on a well-balanced diet should not have any reason to store excess fat.

PROTEINS

Proteins are all-important for your dog's ability to develop and maintain healthy bones, tissues, organs—basically everything. They are made up of compounds called "amino acids," ten of which are not sufficiently produced within the body and must be obtained from food. The best proteins for dogs come from meat, as dogs don't digest plant-based proteins nearly as well as they do animal-based ones. Eggs, fish, meat (such as beef and game), and poultry are all good sources of protein for your Doberman Pinscher.

MINERALS

Minerals fall into two categories: micro and macro. Needed in trace amounts are microminerals, such as iron, zinc, manganese, and copper. Macrominerals, such as calcium, phosphorous, magnesium, and potassium, are needed in greater amounts to keep your Dobie in optimum health.

Before you head to the local health-food store to stock up on mineral supplements, be aware that it can be easy to overdo it. Excess minerals can actually be harmful, throwing off the carefully choreographed dance they perform with other nutrients. If you feel your Dobie could benefit from mineral supplementation, consult a veterinarian or canine nutritionist first.

VITAMINS

Vitamins are compounds important to regular bodily function. A balanced diet should make vitamin supplementation unnecessary, but if certain health conditions require supplementation, proceed only under veterinary guidance.

Vitamins fall into two categories: fat-soluble and water-soluble. Fat-soluble vitamins (A, D, E, and K) are stored in the body's fatty tissue, so daily doses aren't necessary. Water-soluble vitamins (B complex and C) need water for proper absorption. Their frequent replacement is necessary, as any excess is secreted in the urine. Dogs can actually produce vitamin C, which is why you typically won't see it listed on commercial dog food packages.

WATER

The average dog is about two-thirds water. Little wonder that water, which helps regulate body temperature and hydrates muscle tissues, is imperative for good health, let alone survival. This fluid also transports oxygen throughout the body, flushes away certain bacteria, and aids in digestion, keeping things moving smoothly.

A healthy dog should consume .5 to .75 fluid ounces (15 to 22 mL) of water per pound (.5 kg) of body weight each day. This comes from both food and drink. In hot weather or with strenuous exercise, he'll need more. Your Dobie should have constant access to cool, fresh water. If you notice him drinking more than usual, it could be a sign of illness. Consult your veterinarian.

COMMERCIAL FOODS

Commercial dog food reigns as the most popular way to nourish the family dog, as proven by the scads of choices available to consumers. Fortunately, the dog-food industry has recognized that different breeds and life stages require different nutrition, taking much of the guesswork out of feeding your dog. But not all commercial foods are created equal, and there are some things to know before you buy.

DRY FOOD (KIBBLE)

A popular and economical choice, kibble (or "dry food") is a top seller because it can be stored easily without refrigeration and purchased in bulk quantities.

Another advantage is that chewing crunchy kibble can help minimize plaque and tartar buildup on your dog's teeth. (Once plaque hardens into tartar, it cannot be removed except by veterinary intervention.)

But there's a catch to such convenience. To keep costs down, many dog-food manufacturers use lower-quality ingredients: meat by-products, grain hulls, or even substandard meats rated unfit for human consumption. Moreover, since grains cost less than meat does, some dry foods may consist primarily of grain products rather than the animal protein dogs need for a nutritious diet.

Read package labels carefully to determine which brands offer the best-quality food. Look for wholesome animal protein (not meat by-products, which are throwaway parts that have little food value) listed as one of the first four ingredients.

WET FOOD (CANNED)

Canned (or "wet") dog food has high moisture content, which makes eating easier for older dogs who have dental or digestive issues. Canned food's higher fat content also makes it appealing to the dog's palate, but that doesn't necessarily lend itself to optimum nutrition. Neither do the by-products and fillers that often comprise less expensive brands of canned food. Moreover, wet food doesn't provide any of the dental advantages that dry food does, and it may lead toward bad breath, making regular toothbrushing even more important.

Research your options carefully when planning your Doberman's diet.

Wet foods also tend to cost more than other commercial dog foods, and because of their higher water content, you have to feed more to your Dobie in order for him to receive adequate nutrition. That means greater fat intake and pocketbook outgo, neither one of which is a good thing. (Look into comparing foods on a dry-matter basis, however, because the moisture content of canned foods can obscure their nutritional value.)

SEMI-MOIST FOOD

We've all seen them: meaty-looking tidbits shaped like chops, burgers, or bacon strips. Unfortunately, that resemblance is about as close as semi-moist products come to being real food. While their price tag may fool you into thinking you're buying high-quality meat for your dog, these T-bone-shaped treats consist of non-nutritious fillers and artificial flavors and colors.

Semi-moist food tastes good to your dog, but it's basically doggy junk food and doesn't provide any benefits to his dental hygiene. Because these treats promote plaque and tartar buildup, toothbrushing becomes even more important for your dog. And let's face it: your Dobie doesn't care if what he eats is shaped like a steak. All he cares about is whether it's tasty, and all you should care about is whether it meets his nutritional needs.

Noncommercial diets require careful planning to ensure complete nutrition.

Dog Tale

When Saundra B. of Millersville, Maryland, adopted Walter, her adult Doberman, he was about 10 pounds (4.5 kg) overweight. "The family that surrendered him apparently gave him treats every time they turned around," Saundra said. "Fortunately, Walter enjoys the raw carrots and apple slices I give him for treats. I also put him on a 'diet' by giving him slightly smaller portions of senior-formula dog food mixed with salt-free canned green beans. The beans added substance without a lot of calories. Walter lost the excess weight in about six weeks."

NONCOMMERCIAL FOODS

Noncommercial foods are not readily available in supermarkets or convenience stores, but their surge in popularity means that a little homework should turn up a source in your general area, whether it's a butcher shop, a specialty pet-supply store, or food co-op. The noncommercial diet requires more time and effort on your part, but many dog owners feel the benefits are well worth the slight inconvenience.

HOME-COOKED DIET

For those who prefer to be in complete control of their dog's food, the home-cooked diet is a good option. When properly researched and prepared, home-cooked dog food is a great way to ensure that your Dobie is getting the right nutrition.

What's on the menu of a home-cooked diet? Much of the same things we'd eat, minus the carbs. Common items include poultry, beef, salmon or other fish, eggs, and organ meats. Everything should be cooked.

Be warned, though. The home-cooked diet requires forethought, preparation, and commitment. You'll want to take the same precautions preparing your dog's food that you do preparing food for your family. That means properly handling perishable foods, thoroughly cooking meats to prevent digestive upsets from spoiled or undercooked food, and ensuring that each meal provides healthy proportions of required nutrients to make up a balanced diet.

Check your proposed diet with your veterinarian or canine nutritionist to make sure your dog doesn't experience nutrient deficiencies. Then monitor your

Dobie's weight and adjust portions according to his activity level and nutritional needs. Sure, it takes longer than tearing open a bag or opening a can, but doesn't your Doberman Pinscher deserve the best?

RAW DIET

The bones-and-raw-food (or "biologically appropriate raw food") diet, commonly referred to as "the BARF diet," hearkens back to a dog's wild origins. As the name suggests, the BARF diet typically contains 60 to 80 percent raw, meaty bones, with the remainder being a combination of fruits, veggies, eggs, and organ meats. The idea is for your dog to eat the same kinds of food a dog in the wild would eat when hunting. (Since prey animals are typically herbivores, the wild dogs who consume them eat what they have eaten, thus ingesting the small amounts of plant material they need.)

When given a raw diet, dogs eat both meat *and* bones, which contain important minerals like phosphorous. Contrary to popular belief, eating raw poultry bones does not pose a choking hazard. Only cooked bones become brittle and splinter, causing life-threatening problems when ingested. (You should never feed your dog cooked bones.) Raw poultry bones are a crunchy,

PUPPY POINTER

Puppies have different nutritional needs than adult dogs do. These needs govern both what and how often they should eat. The following are some guidelines for feeding your Doberman Pinscher puppy:

- Zero to eight weeks of age: Mother's milk is needed for adequate nutrition and immunity development, but soft dog foods (such as kibble softened with a bit of broth or warm water, canned puppy food, or semi-moist food, if you prefer) can be introduced when puppies are five to six weeks old. Dry puppy foods can be introduced at six to eight weeks.
- Eight weeks to six months of age: Weaning usually takes place between eight and ten weeks. Puppies should be fed at least three times a day until they are six months old.
- Six months to one year of age: At six months old, puppies can begin twice-daily feedings. When they are between ten and twelve months of age, they can begin transitioning to adult-formula dog food.

useful component of raw diets. They help keep teeth and gums clean and are easily digested.

Fans of BARF diets swear by them for their dogs' glossy coats, bright eyes, and energetic good health. As with the home-cooked diet, adequate research and planning are required to ensure that your Dobie avoids nutritional deficiencies.

WHEN TO FEED YOUR DOBERMAN PINSCHER

Doberman Pinscher puppies should eat three to four small meals a day throughout their first six months. After that, split an age-appropriate amount of food between a morning and an early-evening meal. Needless to say, fresh drinking water should be available at all times.

FREE-FEEDING VERSUS SCHEDULED FEEDING

With American obesity at an all-time high, it's pretty clear that we humans have trouble pushing ourselves away from the table when we've eaten sufficiently. So how can we rationally expect our dogs to practice portion control?

Let's face it: given the chance, most dogs will eat until all available food is gone. Which is why free-feeding (leaving dry food out at all times) is not the best idea for your Dobie. He can get sick or obese from overeating, and even if he is the rare dog who will stop eating when satisfied, leaving food out all the time could attract insects or worse critters.

Free-feeding also limits your dog-food choices to kibble. Any other option will dry out or spoil if left unrefrigerated for lengthy periods of time, posing a health threat if consumed.

It's far more sensible to feed your Dobie fresh food at regularly scheduled intervals. Not only does scheduled feeding allow you to control food type and portion size, but it also eliminates the opportunity for your dog to become a picky eater. A dog who understands that meals come only at certain times and for a limited window of opportunity will make the most of each occasion.

OBESITY

Even dogs as naturally sleek and elegant as the Doberman Pinscher can become obese if they overeat. Excess pounds (kg) can also creep on if you give your Doberman food that isn't nutritionally balanced or wholesome, even in moderate amounts. Couple these scenarios with insufficient exercise and you have a Dobie who can easily gain too much weight.

Obesity is a serious issue for dogs, even Doberman Pinschers.

Obesity in dogs is a health hazard for all the same reasons it is in humans: too much stress on the organs and joints, shortness of breath, decreased quality of life. We might think that "food is love," but too much of that kind of love is detrimental to your dog's health.

Not sure how to tell if your Dobie is overweight? Beyond asking your veterinarian, there's an easy way to gauge for yourself. Gently palpate your dog's ribs; they should be readily detected without exerting pressure. The ribs should be visible but not overly prominent—you don't want an underweight Dobie either. If you feel your Dobie is overweight, consult your breeder or veterinarian for advice on the best way to slim him down. Your vet can recommend a good dog food for weight loss and offer exercise tips.

Slow but steady weight loss is best for dogs. Overweight dogs need to build up their fitness programs, so don't expect an obese Dobie to have the same athletic capabilities as one in peak condition. Your best bet, though, is to prevent obesity in the first place. Smart eating, plenty of exercise, and your special brand of TLC will keep your Dobie looking and feeling fit and trim.

GROOMING YOUR
DOBERMAN PINSCHER

The handsome Doberman Pinscher is what we all wish we were: gorgeous-looking all the time with very little effort—no time-consuming trips to the groomer, no special grooming accessories, and no large clumps of shedding hair drifting about the house. But keep in mind that "low maintenance" doesn't equate to "no maintenance."

THE IMPORTANCE OF GROOMING

The minor grooming a Dobie needs is a wonderful way to spend some bonding time with him. What Dobie wouldn't relish a brushing or petting session with his favorite human? Grooming gloves may remove loose, dead hair, but all your Dobie knows is that you're petting him.

Regular grooming, however minimal, is also an excellent way to give your Dobie a once-over for any skin issues or parasites. While you're brushing or currying him, you can check for any fleas or ticks, as well as any irritations or hot spots. Including this as part of your routine will familiarize you with your Dobie's normal, healthy exterior so that you'll be better able to identify any abnormalities in the future.

GROOMING SUPPLIES

Some basic grooming supplies can be found in your own medicine cabinet; other, dog-specific supplies can be found in pet-supply stores. Here's a handy list to get you started.

- **Cotton balls:** Cotton balls are useful for cleaning ears and eyes and for applying ointments.
- **Nail clippers or grinding tool:** Nail clippers come in different sizes, so be sure to get one large enough to handle an adult Dobie's thick nails. Powered grinding tools, also known as Dremels, work on nails of all sizes but may take some patience to get your dog used to the noise and vibration.
- **Shampoo:** Purchase a canine-formulated shampoo for your Dobie. Human shampoos contain detergents that are too drying for a dog's coat, which can lead to irritation and itching. A human shampoo can also dull his shiny coat.
- **Shedding comb:** This tool is a metal loop notched with small teeth that's attached to a handle. As you gently pass the shedding comb over the dog's coat, the teeth grasp loose hair.
- **Soft-bristle brush or grooming glove:** Get a brush with soft, natural bristles or a grooming glove that distributes oils and removes loose, dead hair without being too harsh on the Dobie's skin.
- **Toothbrush or rubber finger sheath:** Purchase a doggy toothbrush or a finger

Dogs wear their coats every day, so keeping them clean and healthy is important to their well-being.

sheath, a latex or rubber cover that fits over your index finger to act like a toothbrush.

- **Toothpaste:** Specially made with canines in mind, dog toothpaste is usually flavored with chicken, bacon, or some other tempting taste. Do not use human toothpaste to brush your dog's teeth; it contains ingredients that can make him sick if ingested, and he won't know that he needs to spit it out.

COAT AND SKIN CARE

Dogs wear their coats every day of their lives, so keeping them clean and healthy is as important to their overall well-being as it is to their appearance. A weekly brushing should suffice to remove dead skin cells and loose hair, but feel free to indulge your Dobie in more frequent brushings. He'll enjoy the attention and the sensation, and you'll enjoy how shiny and beautiful his coat looks and feels.

Although the Doberman Pinscher lacks a thick double coat, he will "blow" his coat twice a year, when he will shed heavily as new growth comes in. For those times, you might find a shedding comb useful. This is best done outside because the fur will fly! You'll be surprised at how much loose hair can be combed out at the height of shedding season, even from a short-coated breed like the Doberman Pinscher.

BRUSHING

How to brush your dog may seem like a no-brainer, but here are some tips to remember that will enhance your Dobie's grooming experience.

How to Brush

1. Brush in the same direction the coat lies, using only gentle pressure.
2. Start at the head and work toward the tail.
3. Remember to brush the legs and underside, using extra-gentle short strokes.
4. Finish with a hug and a kiss for how handsome he looks!

BATHING

The naturally clean Dobie shouldn't require bathing more than a few times a year unless he's a therapy or show dog. (Bathe once a month at most so that your dog's skin doesn't become overly dry.) Regular brushing should loosen and remove any surface dirt he acquires, and baby wipes or grooming towelettes make quick refreshers for those times when he just needs a little extra sprucing up.

Brushing your Doberman with a shedding comb helps remove excess hair.

But there are situations that will call for a full-out bath, which can be a challenge for a dog the size of an adult Dobie. Use a mild, moisturizing dog shampoo.

Where to Bathe

- **Bathtub:** Place a rubber mat in the tub to stabilize his footing, and use a hand-held shower nozzle if possible.
- **Stall shower:** A stall shower is easier than a tub for your Dobie to access, and you may be able to remove the shower head and temporarily attach a hand-held sprayer for the task.
- **Self-serve bathing station:** Many specialty pet businesses feature these bathing areas with spray nozzles, shampoo, towels, and blow dryers, all for a fixed price on a walk-in basis.
- **Mobile groomer:** These grooming vans with bathing facilities on board come to you. What could be easier?
- **Professional groomer:** Veterinary offices and large pet-supply stores usually have on-site bathing services available by appointment.

Getting your dog accustomed to toothbrushing makes the process much easier.

How to Bathe

To make bath time as tolerable as possible for your Dobie, it helps to be organized.

1. Assemble everything you need ahead of time so that you have it all at your fingertips: tub mat, shampoo, towels, and cotton balls.

2. Make sure that the room is sufficiently warm, or bathe outdoors on a warm summer's day.

3. If bathing in a tub or shower, place a rubber mat on the bottom to secure his footing. Adjust the water temperature to a comfortable temperature *before* it touches your Dobie. Fill the tub to a shallow depth.

Dog Tale

Sheila D. of Annapolis, Maryland, laughs that she never had any trouble bathing her Doberman, Bailey. "She loves getting sprayed with cool water from the garden hose," Sheila said. "Every summer I'd be sure to give her a bath outside, soaping her up with dog shampoo and rinsing her off with the hose on a gentle spray. She particularly liked the feel of it on her underbelly. Go figure!"

4. Use treats as a bribe, if necessary, to get your Dobie into the bathtub or shower. He'll be more cooperative if he feels stable.

5. Wet your Dobie thoroughly, topside and underneath. If you don't have a hand-held spray attachment, use a plastic bowl to pour water over his body. Apply a dab of shampoo, add a little water, and work into a lather. Rub gently all over the body, taking care to avoid the eyes and ears.

6. Rinse, rinse, rinse! Residual soap can cause itchy skin and a dull coat, so be sure to rinse out every bit of lather.

7. Towel dry. It may take more than one towel!

8. Dampen a cotton ball with warm water or a drop of baby oil and carefully clean inside the ears and around the eyes.

9. Give your squeaky-clean Dobie a treat!

DENTAL CARE

In the wild, dogs naturally kept their teeth clean by consuming the ligaments, tendons, and bones of their prey. Pet dogs who eat commercial or home-cooked diets need a little help to have plaque buildup removed.

Dental hygiene is just as important for our dogs as it is for us. Poor dental hygiene can cause bad breath, tartar buildup, abscesses, and even systemic infection. Canine dental procedures, including cleanings, must be performed at the veterinarian's office while under general anesthesia, which carries an inherent amount of health risks. So it makes sense to give your Dobie's pearly whites the same attention you do your own. It will save you money and stress in the long run.

Vets advise brushing daily or at least three times a week. The trick is to get your dog accustomed to this procedure so that he thinks of it as a fun interaction and not an unpleasant chore from which he runs.

HOW TO BRUSH

1. To acclimate your dog to toothbrushing, start with a yummy-flavored toothpaste formulated just for dogs. Human toothpaste is *not* dog-digestible and should never be used. Besides, your Dobie will enjoy chicken-flavored toothpaste a lot more than he would spearmint.

2. Stroke the outside of your dog's cheeks with your fingers as a subliminal announcement that his mouth is about to be handled.

3. Get him used to having his teeth rubbed by dabbing some dog toothpaste onto your finger and gently rubbing it on his gums and/or teeth. After a few sessions of this, he should be ready for the actual brushing.

4. Using a finger sheath or a dog toothbrush (available at any pet-supply store), gently brush the most accessible teeth first, using an up-and-down motion. As his comfort level with the process rises, increase the number of teeth you brush until you're doing his whole mouth.

5. Give lots of praise and a dentally-friendly treat for a job well done!

Whether your dog's ears are cropped or naturally floppy, you'll want to ensure that they are always clean and comfortable.

EAR CARE

Whether your Dobie's ears are cropped or naturally floppy, you'll want to ensure that they are always clean and comfortable with a routine inspection, maybe during grooming or cuddling.

A variety of things can cause ear problems, including swimming, food allergies, certain medications, and insect bites. It's fairly easy to tell if something's amiss with your Dobie's ears. First of all, take a whiff. A healthy ear should never smell bad. Next, inspect the ears carefully. A healthy ear should never appear irritated or inflamed. Last, touch the ears. A healthy ear should never feel wet with discharge. If your Dobie develops an itchy or irritated ear, he will likely attempt to rub his head on a cushion or scratch at his ears with a paw. Head shaking is a symptom that something is making him uncomfortable. If your dog experiences any of the ear issues described here, take him to the vet.

Treatment for ear inflammation is not a dog's favorite thing. It usually involves a medicated-wash solution gently squirted into his ear, which he will promptly try to remove by shaking his head and spewing it everywhere but the afflicted area. A drop of baby oil on a cotton ball when your Dobie gets a bath or as needed to remove dirt from the inside of the ears should be enough to keep them clean and healthy.

HOW TO CLEAN THE EARS

1. Put a dab of mineral oil on a few clean cotton balls.
2. Gently hold the ear with one hand, slightly opening the ear flap to expose the ear canal.

3. With an oil-dipped cotton ball in the other hand, gently wipe away any surface dirt inside the ear, using fresh cotton balls as they get dirty. Pay attention to the nooks and crannies, but don't poke down inside the ear. Ear tissues are delicate, and improper or invasive cleaning can cause injury. If you suspect a wax buildup deep inside the ear, don't attempt to purge it yourself. Have the vet take a look and suggest any treatment that may be necessary.
4. Use a clean, dry cotton ball to wipe the ear dry and finish the cleaning.
5. Repeat this process on the other ear.

EYE CARE

It's said that the eyes are windows to the soul, so you want to make sure that your Dobie's beautiful soul shines through!

Because our dogs can't verbalize if they are experiencing any vision changes or eye issues, it's up to us to, well, keep an eye on their eyes. If you need an

Your Dobie's eyes should be clear and free of swelling or inflammation.

extra reason to gaze into those baby browns, here it is. Check for any signs of redness, copious or yellow/green discharge, swelling or inflammation of the lid area, or any behavior that might indicate discomfort: repeated pawing at the eye or rubbing it on the ground or furniture. These are indications that something is wrong, and you should have a vet look at the eye immediately. Cloudy eyes also warrant a professional look. They may be nothing more than signs of normal aging in an adult dog, but you never want to take a chance with your Dobie's eye health.

HOW TO CLEAN THE EYE AREA

A Doberman Pinscher's eye area doesn't require any specialized cleaning, except perhaps to wipe away any normal secretions or "sleep" that accumulates in the corners. A warm, wet washcloth is sufficient to gently wipe away any discharge from his eyes.

HOW TO ADMINISTER EYE DROPS

If your vet has prescribed medicated eye drops for an eye issue, you'll need to learn how to administer them properly. Here are the steps:

1. Talk to your dog in a happy voice and have a treat ready in your pocket.
2. Bring him to a convenient location, preferably where you can place his hindquarters against something so that he can't back away from you.
3. Shake the medication bottle if necessary and uncap it.
4. Place a hand under your dog's chin and gently lift it upward so that his eyes are looking toward the ceiling.
5. Rest your other hand, which is holding the eyedropper, on top of your dog's head. Point the tip of the bottle or dropper away from his eye so that if he jerks, the tip won't poke him in the eye.
6. Holding the dropper or bottle about 1 inch

PUPPY POINTER

Dogs are typically born with five toes and nails: four at the end of each toe on the paw and one higher up on the inner ankle. This is called the dewclaw. Some dogs are born with dewclaws on their rear legs, too, although this isn't as common in Doberman Pinschers as in some other breeds. Dewclaws are positioned too high on the leg to be of much use and have been known to lead to painful injury if the nail catches on an obstacle. Most breeders remove puppies' dewclaws when they are only three to five days old to preclude this possibility.

(2.5 cm) from the eye, squeeze the prescribed number of drops into the eye corner, taking care not to touch the tip to the eye surface.

7. Hold the head for a moment to allow the medication to disperse over the eye. If you don't, your dog will shake his head and much of the medication can fly out of his eye.

8. Give your Dobie the well-deserved treat in your pocket!

NAIL CARE

Keeping your Dobie's nails trimmed to a short length is not just for aesthetic reasons. Nails that are too long can affect a dog's gait and more easily catch on objects (like tree roots), which can tear the nail and cause a painful foot injury. At best, they can inadvertently scratch a dog's humans during play interactions. At worst, overly long nails can curve under the dog's foot and pierce his toe pads.

Dogs in the wild never had to worry about pedicures. Their long daily treks in search of food naturally kept their toenails trim. Today, it's our responsibility to keep their nails trimmed, preferably once a week. Whether you use clippers or a grinding tool, regular nail maintenance should become as routine as brushing your teeth (and your dog's).

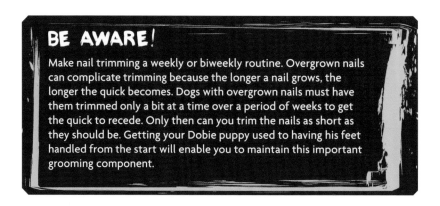

HOW TO TRIM THE NAILS

Because a Doberman Pinscher's nails are black, the biggest concern—accidentally cutting the quick, the blood vessel that runs through the nail—can seem daunting. Here are a few tricks to help you conquer the quick:

1. Have your Dobie lie down on the floor in front of you. Take a paw gently in your hand and observe the curve of the toenail.
2. Shine a flashlight or penlight underneath the nail. The spot where the quick begins should show up darker than the nail edges, giving you a guideline of how far to trim. If you don't have a flashlight available, just trim the curved tip of the nail. You don't have to trim off much, just enough so that his nails don't make a clicking noise when he walks on the floor.
3. If you do accidentally nick the quick, apply some cornstarch or styptic powder to the bleeding nail, or press the nail into a soft bar of soap. The bleeding should stop in short order. But try not to repeat the error. A dog will probably forget and forgive one such mistake, but repeated quick injuries will have him running from nail trimming like the plague.

If fear of cutting the quick really bothers you, consider using a grinding tool (Dremel). It takes a little longer than trimming with clippers, but these tools smooth the nail and reduce the odds of hitting the quick. The biggest challenge with a grinding tool is getting your dog accustomed to it, as the noise can be intimidating. The sensation of the grinder on the nails takes getting used to as well, so the slower the acclimation, the better. Here's how to use a grinding tool:

1. Start by showing the grinder to your Dobie, turning it on and off but not touching the nails. Give him a treat and put it away. Repeat the process several times daily for a few days.

2. Touch his nails with the grinding tool while it's turned off. Apply it with slight pressure to all four paws. Praise and treat. End by briefly turning on the tool so that he remembers what it sounds like. Repeat several times daily until he seems comfortable.

3. Time to grind! Grasp the nail firmly between your fingers to reduce vibration, and gently work the grinder (on high speed; slow speeds cause more vibration) around the nail tip, sculpting as you go and praising all the while. Keep the grinder in motion to prevent discomfort. Do a little bit on each nail, returning for more grinding as needed.

HOW TO FIND A PROFESSIONAL GROOMER

Although the Doberman Pinscher's sleek, short coat makes extensive grooming unnecessary, some people prefer to use a professional groomer for baths and pedicures.

Professional groomers work in veterinary clinics, pet-supply stores, and even out of mobile units that come to your home. As with any professional who provides care or services to your Dobie, you want to find the best one for you and your dog. So how do you go about finding the right groomer?

1. Observe potential groomers at facilities that allow customers to watch them at work. Do they handle their canine clients with compassion and respect? Do they seem to enjoy what they're doing?

2. Ask for referrals. Your neighbors, friends, and fellow Doberman Pinscher owners may have just the beautician for your Dobie. You can also ask your vet to recommend an outside groomer, although most veterinary practices provide the basic grooming services a Dobie needs.

3. When possible, check out the equipment your chosen groomer uses. If a bath is in order, find out if the dryer has adjustable settings. Dryers that are powerful enough for a Siberian Husky may be too hot for a Doberman Pinscher. Also, ask which shampoos and/or flea dips they use. "Gentle" and "environmentally friendly" are important watchwords.

CHAPTER 6

HEALTH OF YOUR
DOBERMAN PINSCHER

Keeping your Doberman Pinscher healthy isn't always as simple as good nutrition and tender loving care. Not only are dogs unable to articulate when they don't feel right, but they often hide symptoms of illness or injury because instinct tells them that a sick dog is a vulnerable dog. That's why it's so important to observe your Dobie on an ongoing basis: you'll be able to clue in when things just aren't quite right.

Whether by consumption (yuck!) of feces, contact with infected dogs, or even everyday mosquito bites, dogs can contract various diseases and parasites. Luckily, Dobies aren't always the most stoic of dogs. Many make it quite plain when they don't feel well. Once you notice a problem, of course, the next step is to get it checked out. Finding a veterinarian you trust is one of your most important responsibilities as a dog owner.

Annual checkups help ensure your Doberman's well-being.

FINDING A VET

Since one of the first things you'll do with your Dobie is get him a veterinary evaluation, your vet finding mission begins even before you bring him home. Personal referrals, especially from other Doberman owners, are a great way to find a trustworthy veterinarian. You can also check the American Animal Hospital Association's (AAHA) website (aaha.org) for AAHA-accredited veterinary hospitals.

Once you've narrowed your search, it's important to ask the right questions, both of the vet candidate and of yourself. For example:
- Is this veterinarian compassionate and dedicated?
- Is she experienced with Doberman Pinschers or at least familiar with Dobie-specific health conditions?
- Is her practice open on evenings and weekends?
- Are there boarding and emergency services on-site? Is someone on-site 24/7 to monitor overnight patients and boarders?

- Is this vet open to answering all your questions?
- Is she current on all the latest veterinary developments?
- Does your dog seem comfortable with her?
- Are you comfortable with the way she handles your dog?

Take your time, select carefully, and you'll soon find a vet who will become an important member of your Dobie's inner circle.

ANNUAL VET VISIT

Taking your Doberman for an annual checkup is just as vital as getting one for yourself. Wait, you don't get an annual checkup? Well, make sure that your Dobie does! It's one of the easiest, most effective ways to support his well-being. An annual wellness exam can pick up on things you may have missed in your own observations. The vet will examine and check for most of the same things your own doctor does, plus a few more.

- abdominal masses
- body temperature
- eyes and ears
- heart and lungs
- lumps, bumps, or signs of discomfort
- teeth and gums for tartar buildup or inflammation
- weight

Depending on her findings, your veterinarian may recommend a blood workup or urinalysis. Stool samples are often requested at annual wellness exams to test for the presence of any internal parasites.

PUPPY POINTER

Even if your new puppy has just visited the breeder's vet, take him for an introductory visit to yours. It's a good idea for your puppy and vet to get acquainted when there are no invasive exams or procedures to be done. Then your pup won't equate the vet with unpleasant things. Wind up the outing with something fun, like a brief walk in the park or a visit to the pet store for a treat. First impressions count!

VACCINATIONS

The subject of vaccinating against disease (for both people and pets) has become controversial in recent years. Opponents to dog vaccination run the gamut, from claiming that introducing toxins into the body is dangerous to saying that dogs who live primarily indoors are not exposed to dangerous diseases and don't need vaccination.

Whatever your take on the subject, vaccinations have been split into two categories: core and noncore. Core vaccinations are considered crucial to a dog's well-being. They protect against potentially fatal diseases, including canine adenovirus, distemper, parvovirus, and rabies. Noncore vaccines protect against illnesses, such as bordetella, coronavirus, and leptospirosis, that may be limited to certain areas or to dogs in certain situations.

According to the AAHA's 2011 canine vaccination guidelines, puppies should receive their adenovirus, distemper, and parvovirus vaccinations in three sets between their 8th and 16th weeks. The legally required rabies vaccine is given when they are at least 12 weeks of age. Your puppy will most likely have already had his first set of shots by the time you bring him home, but it's quite possible you will be responsible for obtaining the others (the breeder should provide you with all pertinent health records and paperwork). This is another reason why your first new-puppy vet visit is all-important.

BORDETELLA (KENNEL COUGH)

This highly contagious respiratory illness gets its common name from one of the places where it spreads to epidemic proportions: boarding kennels. While *Bordetella bronchiseptica* bacteria cause kennel cough, several other infectious agents can be kennel cough culprits as well, usually canine adenovirus type 2 and canine parainfluenza. The symptoms resemble a bad cold or bronchitis, and while not severe, bordetella can quickly spread in environments where large numbers of dogs are kept. Treatment is usually limited to prescription cough suppressants, since the disease has to run its own course. Prevention with an injected vaccine or nasal spray is not only advised—it's now required by most boarding and day-care facilities.

CANINE ADENOVIRUS

Canine adenovirus comes in two forms, and both can be prevented with the CAV-2 vaccine. More frequently affecting dogs less than one year old, canine adenovirus type 1 (CAV-1) causes infectious canine hepatitis. Found worldwide, CAV-1 is spread primarily by bodily fluids. Early symptoms may include a sore throat, coughing, and pneumonia. As CAV-1 enters the bloodstream, it can affect the eyes, liver, and kidneys. As liver and kidney failure ensue, seizures may occur, along with increased thirst, vomiting, and diarrhea.

The horror of CAV-1 is the speed at which it can progress. Death can result as early as two hours after symptoms appear. There is also no specific veterinary treatment; symptoms can only be managed. Intravenous fluid, for

Some vaccinations are essential for your dog, while others depend on his lifestyle.

example, will combat the dehydration caused by vomiting and diarrhea. A dog with sufficient antibodies will recover in a few weeks.

Canine adenovirus type 2 (CAV-2) causes respiratory disease. It's one of the most common contributors to kennel cough, often in conjunction with other viruses or bacteria. Symptoms include coughing, fever, and a runny nose—just what you'd expect from a respiratory illness. Although not serious in and of itself, it is highly contagious and can cause serious problems for older dogs or dogs with already-compromised immune systems.

CORONAVIRUS

Coronavirus is a multistrain viral infection of the intestinal lining that can cause lethargy, loss of appetite, and orange-tinted diarrhea. Transmission is through direct contact with feces or the affected dog. Although no cure is available, most cases recover fully. Fatalities are rare. Treatment includes fluids for dehydration caused by diarrhea and antibiotics for secondary bacterial infections.

DISTEMPER

Distemper can be a devastating disease to unvaccinated dogs. In fact, it's considered their greatest threat. Symptoms vary, but they can include loss of appetite, coughing, fever, diarrhea, vomiting, and lethargy, among others. Early treatment of this highly contagious disease increases the chances for survival, but you know what they say about an ounce of prevention . . . Treatments include antibiotics, antidiarrheal medications, anticonvulsants, and antinauseants. The majority of puppies who contract distemper do not survive, so vaccination against this terrible disease is imperative.

LEPTOSPIROSIS
Caused by *Leptospira* bacteria (spirochetes often carried by rats), leptospirosis attacks the kidneys and liver, causing bloody stools or urine, fever, depression, loss of appetite, reddened eyes and mouth, thirst, painful mouth sores, and pain with movement. Several strains of bacteria can cause this disease, and their prevalence varies in different geographic areas. Vaccination will lessen the severity of the disease but will not prevent it, so your vet can advise you if she feels that vaccination against leptospirosis is warranted. Treatment is usually with antibiotics and should be performed as early as possible, since leptospirosis is transmissible to humans.

Doberman Pinschers are considered more at risk of contracting parvovirus than other dog breeds.

PARVOVIRUS

Parvo is a highly contagious intestinal virus that can prove fatal two or three days after symptoms first appear. Spread through contact with the feces of infected dogs, it can cause listlessness, anorexia, fever, vomiting, and diarrhea. For reasons not yet understood, Doberman Pinschers seem to be at a higher risk than other breeds for contracting parvovirus. There is no cure for this devastating disease, so prevention is essential. Palliative treatments include antinauseants, antibiotics, and intravenous fluids.

RABIES

This very contagious, virus-borne disease attacks the nervous system, causing fearful symptoms that have become legendary: increased salivation, aversion to water, changes in disposition, facial tics, and more. Greatly feared because of its transmissibility to humans, rabies is passed via the bite of an infected animal. Thanks to rabies vaccinations being legally required for domestic animals, the odds of a person contracting rabies from a pet is fairly low. Rabies is known to be carried by bats, raccoons, and foxes, however, which is why it's a good idea to keep your distance from wild animals.

PARASITES

Parasites fall into two groups, external and internal. You don't want either type thinking that your Dobie makes the perfect host. Most will at least make your dog uncomfortable (though some can be carried without his knowledge). At worst, they can kill him. These are squatters you definitely want to evict, or better yet, prevent from staking their claim in the first place.

EXTERNAL PARASITES

These annoying freeloaders, which include parasites such as fleas, ticks, and mites, often attach themselves to your dog's hair or skin, sucking his blood to feed and generally making his life miserable.

Fleas

Fleas jump onto passing hosts and make their homestead, reproducing quickly and causing itchiness where they bite. Some dogs have severe allergic reactions to flea bites, making the problem worse. And the resultant scratching leads to problems of its own, not to mention signaling the potential infestation of your home and family.

There are many options for ridding your dog of fleas, from flea dips at the vet's office to homeopathic remedies like herbal oils. Talk to your veterinarian about

Topical preventives can help your dog avoid catching fleas and other pests.

the best method of prevention so that you and your Dobie don't have to endure these unwelcome guests. One popular option is the topical flea preventive, which provides long-term protection with one application.

Mites

Several types of mites have been known to demonize dogs. Ear mites are infinitesimal critters that typically invade the ear canal, producing a rust-brown, sometimes smelly discharge and irritating your Dobie's sensitive ears. Dogs bothered by ear mites will paw at their ears or rub their head on the ground to relieve the itch.

Mange mites cause more widespread symptoms. Sarcoptic mites cause sarcoptic mange, raising little bumps on the skin and making it itchy and crusty. Demodectic mites infest the hair follicles, causing demodectic mange, which may or may not itch but causes bare patches in the fur. Many dogs have demodectic mites and show no symptoms, however. As such, demodectic mange primarily signals other health problems.

If you suspect that your Doberman Pinscher suffers from ear or mange mites, have the vet check him immediately to determine which mites are the culprits and how to treat them.

Ringworm

Ringworm is neither a worm nor a bloodsucker. It's a fungus that spreads easily among animals and humans alike. Ringworm fungi feed on dead skin cells and hair cells, causing irritating itchiness and scaly bald patches. Puppies and dogs with weak immune systems are most at risk of contracting ringworm.

The ringworm fungus can be tenacious and hard to eliminate, living for years in the environment and resisting treatment, which is usually a combination of systemic and topical medication. The affected dog's environment must also be treated to kill the ringworm spores.

Ticks

Ticks are disease-carrying arachnids that burrow their mouths into a host's skin and suck his blood to feed. Totally nasty. They itch and irritate, making their host uncomfortable and exposing him to illnesses such as Lyme disease and Rocky Mountain spotted fever. They also come in a wide variety of species, with the brown dog tick and the tiny deer tick, carrier of Lyme disease, being the most commonly known varieties.

Doberman Pinscher owners are lucky in that the breed's short, smooth coat makes tick detection that much easier. Ticks are often visible as disruptions in the otherwise sleek coat, and they are readily felt with your hands. However, some

Have your dog tested for heartworm each year before administering his annual heartworm preventives.

kinds, such as the deer tick, can be as small as poppy seeds, making detection more challenging.

Tick prevention should be discussed with your vet as a year-round regimen. Some long-term topical flea preventives also protect against ticks. Give your Dobie a manual and visual check after walks in grassy or wooded areas. If you see him scratching repeatedly at a particular area, give him a good going-over.

INTERNAL PARASITES

The aptly named Animal Planet television program *Monsters Inside Me* says it all: internal parasites can be damaging and sometimes deadly. Modern hygiene practices have made their infestation of humans a rarity in many countries, but with dogs, it's another story.

Heartworms

Heartworms are deadly internal parasites transmitted by mosquito bites. When an infested mosquito bites a dog, it injects him with heartworm larvae. The larvae invade the dog's circulatory system, making their way to the heart, where they mature into adult worms up to 12 inches (30.5 cm) long and start to reproduce. An infested dog can have hundreds of heartworms.

It can be a full six months after the mosquito bite before the worms mature, and even longer before symptoms, such as chronic coughing, weight loss, and fatigue, appear. By this time, serious organ damage may have already been done. Heart failure will ultimately take the dog's life. Treatment for heartworm exists, but it's costly, lengthy, and risky (though arguably not as dangerous as heartworms themselves). Treatment kills the adult heartworms, but dead worms in the heart can then cause a fatal blood clot.

The good news is that heartworms are largely preventable. It's important, however, to test for their presence before administering the preventive. Infested dogs can become seriously ill from the very medication that prevents infestation. And since heartworm prevention isn't completely foolproof, there's always a slight chance that a dog on a preventive regimen can become infested. Since the last thing you want to do is inadvertently make your dog sick, annual heartworm tests are strongly recommended and usually required before your veterinarian writes a new prescription for a heartworm preventive.

Hookworms

These little bloodsuckers literally hook into your dog's intestinal walls to feed, relocating about six times a day. Because the host dog loses blood every time the

hookworms reposition themselves, anemia is a common development. Symptoms of infestation include dark stools, weight loss, general weakness, and pale skin. Transmission is through infested feces. Deworming treatment usually takes care of the problem, while severe cases may need plasma transfusions.

Roundworms

Roundworms are the most common intestinal parasite found in dogs, especially puppies. They can grow up to 7 inches (18 cm) long and cause lethargy, diarrhea, and vomiting. Roundworms are visible as spaghetti strands in the stools of a heavily infested dog, or their eggs will show up in fecal tests. Transmission is through contaminated feces or soil or from pregnant females to their litters. All puppies should be treated for roundworms with deworming products available at pet-supply stores or through your veterinarian.

Tapeworms

These flat, segmented worms grow up to 6 inches (15 cm) long in your dog's small intestine. Fleas that have ingested tapeworm eggs transmit the parasite when they are ingested themselves by their host. Often no symptoms appear unless the dog is severely infested. Then he may experience abdominal discomfort, weight loss, and vomiting. Infestation is usually detected when worm segments are noticed in the dog's stools or around the anus. These are actually egg casings and look like small bits of confetti. See your vet for proper treatment, as over-the-counter treatments don't do the trick for this nasty parasite.

Whipworms
These tiny worms with long, whip-like tails embed into a dog's large intestine, where they feed on his blood. They don't consume as much as hookworms, though, so symptoms often don't appear. Sometimes there will be weight loss or diarrhea. Transmission is through consumption of whipworm eggs found in contaminated feces or soil. As with tapeworms, whipworms require veterinary treatment.

SPAYING/NEUTERING
Responsible dog owners are encouraged to spay or neuter their pets for the most obvious reason: population control. But there are other advantages as well. Spayed female dogs are considered to be at lower risk for breast cancer. If they've had a complete ovariohysterectomy (removal of ovaries and uterus), they obviously are at no risk for ovarian or uterine cancer either. A spayed female will not go into heat, which means no mess for you and no ardent suitors for her.

Neutered males no longer have their testosterone source (their testicles), which means less roaming and urine marking. Plus, they won't respond to a female's pheromones, the scent stimuli that otherwise alert them to females in season. Without this distraction, they will stay more focused during training. And obviously, testicular cancer is not a risk for neutered males.

In the United States, most dogs are neutered between five and eight months of age. Although some veterinarians will neuter a dog as young as six weeks old, that doesn't mean younger is better. There's a lot to be said for allowing a puppy to develop normally before altering his system. Females are best spayed around nine

Waiting until your dog is more mature before spaying or neutering can promote better health.

months of age, when they're old enough to better tolerate general anesthesia, which is required for the surgery, but before they experience their first estrus. Seek advice from your breeder or veterinarian as to the best time to spay or neuter your dog.

BREED-SPECIFIC ILLNESSES

Every breed is prone to certain genetic disorders, and the Doberman Pinscher is no exception. This doesn't mean that every Dobie is destined to develop one or more of these disorders; it just means that some are more prevalent in some breeds than in others.

Careful breeding goes a long way toward eliminating unwanted genes from future generations. Therefore, choosing the right breeder requires thoughtful research if you want to reduce the potential for inherited health issues in the Dobie you ultimately add to your family. Let's take a look at some of the more common inherited conditions found in the Doberman Pinscher.

ENTROPION

Entropion involves the inward rolling of the eyelid, which causes the eyelashes to continually irritate the eye. Symptoms include excessive tearing, squinting, and discharge. Surgery is the only way to rectify this condition, but the success rate is high. Without surgery, a dog with entropion will not only be uncomfortable but may develop scarred or ulcerated corneas that will permanently affect his vision.

HIP DYSPLASIA

This is one of the most common joint problems for larger dog breeds, and the Doberman Pinscher falls into the at-risk category. Hip dysplasia occurs when the ball at the end of the femur (thigh bone) doesn't fit properly into the hip socket. The femur then moves out of place, causing friction and pain. Symptoms may include difficulty rising, lying down, or jumping; lameness; and skipping with the hind legs while running.

Hip dysplasia can present at any age but is definitely treatable. Mild cases can be managed with medications, while severe cases may need corrective surgery. Reputable breeders will have their breeding stock tested for hip dysplasia and certified free of the condition by the Orthopedic Foundation for Animals (OFA). You greatly reduce your chances of acquiring a Dobie with a genetic tendency toward this disease if you look for this certification in the parents.

Good breeders carefully screen their dogs to reduce each puppy's chances of genetic conditions.

PROGRESSIVE RETINAL ATROPHY (PRA)

Progressive retinal atrophy (PRA) damages the retina, eventually causing total blindness. The first sign will be either night blindness or reduced vision in dim light. As PRA worsens, the pupils become dilated and cataracts may develop. Unfortunately, there is no cure or correction for this devastating condition.

SKIN DISORDERS

The Doberman Pinscher is known to suffer from a disproportionate number of skin and pigment disorders, such as color-dilution alopecia, demodicosis, and hypopigmentation (albinism).

Color-dilution alopecia usually occurs in dogs bred for unusual colors. In Doberman Pinschers, it applies to fawn, a dilution of red or brown, and blue, a dilution of black, coats. Color-dilution alopecia can cause permanent patchy hair loss or scaly skin but doesn't really affect the dog's quality of life.

Demodicosis occurs when a young or deficient immune system allows demodectic mites to overpopulate, causing patchy hair loss. The dog usually outgrows this condition, and the mites are easily treated.

Hypopigmentation (albinism) in Dobermans is sometimes restricted to the muzzle, resulting in pink noses or lips, which would ordinarily be dark. With complete albinism, the Doberman's fur is white (or partially white with freckles or light shades of pigment). Affected dogs are often light-sensitive and more susceptible to sunburn and skin cancer. Don't be fooled by people marketing white Doberman Pinschers as "rare" or "unusual" (i.e., more valuable). These dogs have genetic anomalies and should never be allowed to reproduce.

WOBBLER SYNDROME

As the name implies, this hereditary condition gives affected dogs a wobbly appearance. This results from abnormalities in the vertebrae, disks, or ligaments of the neck that compress the spinal cord and cause weakness and incoordination. Dobermans and Great Danes seem to be most commonly affected. Treatments include neck braces to restrict neck movement and anti-inflammatory medications to prevent permanent spinal cord damage. They are more managerial than recuperative.

GENERAL ILLNESSES

While certain illnesses seem to be prevalent within certain breeds or breed groups, most health conditions can affect any dog. Doberman Pinschers are

Doberman Pinschers are known to suffer from various skin conditions.

as much at risk as any dog for some common health issues, many of which were once death sentences. But thanks to advances in veterinary medicine and greater awareness of holistic remedies, many afflicted dogs have second chances at full lives.

ALLERGIES

Allergies have reached epidemic proportions these days in both animals and humans. We humans may sneeze, break out in hives, and have watery eyes. Dogs with allergies typically experience similar problems, which are as bothersome to them as our stuffy noses are to us. Canine allergies can be grouped into four categories: flea, inhalant, food, and contact.

- **Flea allergies:** The most common type of allergy in dogs, the flea allergy isn't to the flea itself but to a protein in its saliva left in your dog's skin after a bite. Typical reactions include itchiness and small inflamed bumps. When severe, this allergy can make the poor dog miserable.
- **Inhalant allergies:** The second most common variety, inhalant allergies are triggered when a dog breathes in an offending allergen, such as pollen, tobacco smoke, or mold spores. These allergens can find their way into your house from outdoors, so the "indoor dog" isn't immune to them (and at any rate, Doberman Pinschers shouldn't be strictly "indoor dogs"). If your dog seems to suffer from a runny nose, itchy or runny eyes, or excessive sneezing or coughing, consult your vet for advice on treatment.
- **Food allergies:** Many foods that cause allergies in humans can have the same effect on dogs. Soy, milk products, eggs, wheat, corn, and chicken are commonly seen food allergens. The most likely reaction is itchy, irritated skin, although vomiting and diarrhea may occur. Trial and error is often the only way to isolate a food allergen, but once the problem has been identified, it is a simple matter to adjust the dog's diet accordingly.
- **Contact allergies:** These allergies manifest when the affected dog touches substances containing the allergen. Symptoms include chronic itchiness,

Allergy treatment can be as simple as changing your dog's diet or as involved as getting him immunotherapy.

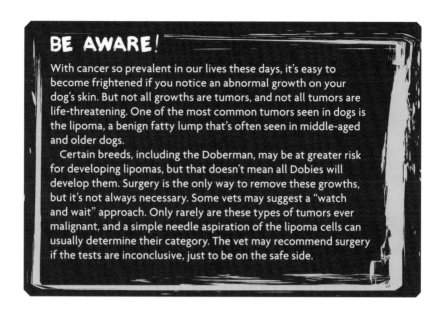

BE AWARE!

With cancer so prevalent in our lives these days, it's easy to become frightened if you notice an abnormal growth on your dog's skin. But not all growths are tumors, and not all tumors are life-threatening. One of the most common tumors seen in dogs is the lipoma, a benign fatty lump that's often seen in middle-aged and older dogs.

Certain breeds, including the Doberman, may be at greater risk for developing lipomas, but that doesn't mean all Dobies will develop them. Surgery is the only way to remove these growths, but it's not always necessary. Some vets may suggest a "watch and wait" approach. Only rarely are these types of tumors ever malignant, and a simple needle aspiration of the lipoma cells can usually determine their category. The vet may recommend surgery if the tests are inconclusive, just to be on the safe side.

hair loss, and skin changes like rashes or hives. Allergy shots often ease the uncomfortable symptoms, but lifestyle changes may be necessary. A Dobie who is allergic to plastic should eat and drink from bowls of another material. One who's allergic to grass has a bigger challenge, since alternative relaxation and recreational surfaces must be provided. I'm sure your Dobie wouldn't mind giving up a nap in the backyard in exchange for a place on the sofa!

Treatments for occasional flare-ups include shots and medications, such as steroids or antihistamines. For ongoing issues, however, dog owners should investigate other methods of coping, such as immunotherapy. Immunotherapy is designed to desensitize the dog by building up his immunity to an allergen through injecting small amounts of it or its extracts (the same principle behind homeopathy). Many dogs have been known to respond well to this treatment.

CANCER

As rampant among dogs as it is among humans, cancer has been considered the number-one most common fatal disease in purebred dogs. Half of all dogs who die over the age of ten die of cancer, and nearly half of all dogs who die from a natural disease die of cancer.

Studies have shown that one in five dogs will develop cancer, which becomes a greater risk with age. While all dogs are susceptible, some also have genetic predispositions. As with people, lighter-skinned dogs are at greater risk for skin cancer, but this common form can strike any dog at any time.

Early detection can extend your dog's life or even save it, so be observant for warning signs. Feel his body for unusual growths. Take note of his appetite and water intake. Monitor his energy level and general mood. If he hasn't been feeling well, it doesn't mean that he has cancer, so don't expect the worst. Just have the vet give him a thorough checkup.

Gloomy statistics notwithstanding, you can take steps to reduce your dog's chances of developing cancer. Decreasing his exposure to toxins like secondhand smoke, harmful chemicals, and artificial ingredients can help. A healthy lifestyle including wholesome food and plenty of exercise is crucial. Preventive measures and ever-improving treatments offer hope for future canine generations.

GASTRIC TORSION (BLOAT)

Gastric torsion (or "bloat") is a serious condition that can affect any breed, but it most commonly seems to affect larger breeds. Bloat occurs when the dog's stomach becomes distended from gas, water, or both, swelling and sometimes twisting (known as "torsion"). An otherwise healthy dog can die a painful death from gastric torsion in a matter of hours, so it should be taken very seriously.

When bloat occurs, the esophagus closes off, limiting the dog's ability to relieve stomach distention by vomiting or belching, and the stomach becomes as taut as a drum, causing severe pain. The distended abdomen pushes against the lungs, making breathing difficult, and presses on the caudal vena cava, the large vessel transporting blood from the abdominal area to the heart. When this blood flow is restricted, heart failure is inevitable. Emergency surgery is the only way to save the dog's life.

The symptoms of bloat are distinctive: abdominal pain and swelling; a dazed, stunned expression; excessive drooling and panting; pacing and restless attempts to find a cool place to lie down; pale gums; and repetitive but futile attempts to vomit. If you notice any of these symptoms in your Dobie, stay calm and get immediate veterinary help. Time is of the essence in order to save the bloated dog's life.

Studies have shown that certain external factors can contribute to bloat. Some risk factors include the following: eating too fast or gulping water; gender and age (males and dogs over the age of two seem to be more often affected); mealtime agitation and stress; and strenuous exercise right after eating or drinking.

HEART DISEASE

Heart disease can affect any breed. Sometimes related to an unhealthy lifestyle, it can also occur subsequent to other issues. Common symptoms

Dobermans are prone to dilated cardiomyopathy, but early detection can slow its progression.

include coughing, fatigue, and restlessness before bed. While heart disease causes serious problems, veterinary care can help affected dogs lead longer, more enjoyable lives.

One form known to affect the Doberman Pinscher is dilated cardiomyopathy, which causes enlargement of the heart chambers. This can result in irregular heart rhythms, fluid buildup inside the lungs, and congestive heart failure, wherein the heart cannot pump enough blood and internal leaking occurs. In approximately 17 percent of affected dogs, sudden death is the first and only symptom. Dogs who experience prior symptoms may suffer dramatic weight loss, and their irregular heart rhythms can provoke episodes of extreme weakness or collapse. By the time these symptoms appear, usually in middle-aged dogs, the prognosis may already be gloomy.

Early detection, however, has been shown to slow the progression of the disease. Regular checkups can help veterinarians detect irregular heart rhythms. If dilated cardiomyopathy is suspected, further testing can confirm. Treatment varies, but heart medications and lifestyle modifications can improve the affected dog's quality of life and longevity. Even with congestive heart failure, treatments are often available.

ALTERNATIVE THERAPIES

While many swear by traditional veterinary medicine, alternative approaches to animal health care have become more mainstream. Chiropractic, acupuncture, herbal therapy, and homeopathy (along with practices like reiki) complement traditional treatments and appeal to those seeking a more holistic approach to their Doberman Pinscher's well-being.

ACUPUNCTURE

Acupuncture involves sticking needles (painlessly) into the skin along the body at access points where energy accumulates. This is said to unblock energy flow, which promotes healing. Traditionally a Chinese technique, acupuncture has become well known and readily available around the world for both people and pets. Holistic veterinarians practice this therapy as a companion treatment for a variety of health issues, and many dog owners swear by the results.

CHIROPRACTIC

From the Greek for "hand practice," chiropractic treatment concerns the relationship of the spinal column to the nervous and circulatory systems as well as to biomechanics and movement. People often associate this therapy merely with relieving back pain, but chiropractors also manipulate the vertebrae to alter disease progression and relieve joint, nerve, and muscle problems.

HERBAL THERAPY

Herbs, the most basic form of medicine available, have been used for their curative properties for thousands of years. They treat a wide variety of physical, emotional, and mental ailments, as we can see in the popularity of St. John's wort for depression, black cohosh for menopause side effects, and lavender as aromatherapy for tension and insomnia.

Alternative therapies can complement traditional treatments.

Herbs are used to help dogs with everything from bad breath to separation anxiety. Professional herbalists know which substances have been successful in treating canine conditions, but you should always check with your veterinarian before administering herbal treatments. An otherwise harmless herb may negate or adversely interact with pharmaceuticals your dog is taking. Also be aware of side effects or allergic reactions your Dobie may experience to an herbal treatment. While traditional veterinarians may put more stock in the science of pharmacology than in herbal therapies, they ultimately have your dog's best interest at heart and should be open to discussing complementary treatment.

HOMEOPATHY

Homeopathy is based on the principle that "like cures like," so homeopathic specialists formulate remedies for symptoms caused by the remedy's primary ingredient. If syrup of ipecac induces vomiting, a homeopathic remedy for nausea and vomiting might contain ipecac. The very ingredient that causes vomiting is used to alleviate it.

Homeopathic medicines are highly diluted forms of the original substance said to stimulate the patient's life force to begin the healing process. With holistic veterinarians becoming more and more prevalent, veterinary homeopathy may soon be considered a helpful companion to conventional medicine.

FIRST AID

Accidents happen, and emergencies require urgent action. Knowing what to do beforehand can help you save your dog stress and harm. The following are some common emergency situations for dogs.

HEATSTROKE

Heatstroke is a deadly condition that results from overheating, typically in hot weather or from being inside an enclosed vehicle outside in warm weather. During heatstroke, the dog's body temperature soars; he may vomit, have difficulty breathing, or collapse. If you suspect your Dobie is suffering from heatstroke, take immediate action. Lower his body temperature by placing him in a tub of cool (not cold) water or wrapping him in a cool, wet towel. Then take him immediately to the vet or emergency room.

Common sense can easily prevent heatstroke. During outdoor exercise in hot weather, make sure your Dobie has shade and plenty of fresh water available. If the temperature or heat index is extreme, save the park for a cooler day. And

BE AWARE!

Having a well-stocked, up-to-date first-aid kit handy goes a long way toward facilitating your peace of mind if and when the need arises. How elaborate the kit will be is your choice, but the following basics should be included:

- antihistamine tablets (with dosage guidelines)
- antiseptic ointment
- cotton balls and swabs
- gauze pads and rolls of elasticized, self-adhesive gauze
- hydrogen peroxide
- large towel or blanket
- pet-first-aid manual (for emergencies like choking, arterial bleeding, etc.)
- petroleum jelly
- rectal thermometer
- scissors
- sterile saline eye wash
- tweezers

Keep the kit fully stocked and replace expired substances and unusable supplies as needed. Also include contact information for your veterinarian, your nearest emergency veterinary medical center, and ASPCA Animal Poison Control ([888] 426-4435).

never leave your dog in a parked car, even on a moderately warm day, even with the windows open.

HYPOTHERMIA AND FROSTBITE

Dogs can experience complications from cold weather as well as they can from warm. These include hypothermia and frostbite. The Doberman's short coat will not offer him much protection against freezing temperatures, so it's especially important to keep him warm to avoid the following conditions.

Hypothermia is the other side of the heatstroke coin, a lower-than-normal body temperature resulting from exposure to very cold environments. How do you know if your dog is hypothermic? If you see him shivering, limping, or behaving lethargically, he may be in trouble. Safely raise his body temperature by moving him to a warm area and covering him with a blanket. Hot water bottles or hot packs wrapped in towels are also useful for warming.

Frostbite, characterized by stiff or blackened appendages, damages the tissues of the extremities. If you suspect frostbite, move your dog to a warmer place and warm the affected area with a towel soaked in lukewarm water. Don't try to rub or massage the frostbitten area, as this can damage tissues.

After providing responsive treatment, seek immediate veterinary attention for either situation. You can help prevent hypothermia and frostbite by limiting your Dobie's exposure to very cold temperatures or wind chills. If he must be outdoors in winter weather, protect him with outer garments and booties.

POISONING

Any time your dog consumes a substance that is toxic to his system, poisoning can occur. Common causes of accidental pet poisoning include toxic foods and plants, antifreeze, cleaning products, and medications. Symptoms include vomiting, diarrhea, coordination loss, drooling, and seizures.

Because some toxic substances do even more damage when vomiting is induced, never attempt to do so without first contacting your vet or the ASPCA's 24-hour Animal Poison Control hotline at (888) 426-4435. If you know what substance caused the poisoning, have product information ready to provide to the professionals. In case you *are* instructed to induce vomiting, it's a good idea to keep some hydrogen peroxide or ipecac syrup handy.

SENIOR DOBERMANS

Unfortunately, the larger the breed, the shorter the life span. The Doberman Pinschers become senior citizens when they are around nine years old. Of course,

Dog Tale

If you've never been to the emergency veterinary clinic in your area, you might want to make a dry run when you aren't under stress. When my own dog had a sudden anaphylactic reaction to an insect bite at 11:00 p.m. on a Sunday evening, I had to rush her to the emergency clinic while she was having difficulty breathing. It was about 20 minutes away and off the beaten path, so if I hadn't gone there once before just to check it out, I could have easily missed it. With every moment counting toward saving my dog's life, I would not have wanted to waste precious time trying to find a location with which I was unfamiliar.

age is but a number, and thanks to better diets and modern veterinary care, dogs can live longer than ever before. While that means you'll have your beloved companion around as long as possible, it also means there will be age-related issues you must deal with.

Senior dogs aren't so very different from senior humans. Their metabolisms slow down, their hearing and sight can deteriorate, their skin can experience changes, and joint degeneration is inevitable to some degree. This means tweaking a few things in your routine.

DIETARY CHANGES

As your Dobie gets older, his diet should have a lower fat (but not protein) content, so consider switching to dog food formulated for seniors. Senior foods often include lamb and rice, which are gentle on the senior stomach. Should your Dobie develop a sensitive stomach, probiotics can help regulate his digestive system. These are widely available over the counter (check with your veterinarian regarding dosage).

Of course, you've been taking good care of your Doberman's oral hygiene, but even a healthy mouth can experience sensitivity with age. You may need to soften your Dobie's food with water or add canned food to make chewing easier. Gum issues are common in older dogs, so be sure his mouth is thoroughly checked during his annual veterinary visit.

PHYSICAL DISCOMFORT

Because joints naturally degenerate with age, arthritis is a common problem for older dogs. You may notice your Dobie having a harder time getting up or lying down. He may shy away from jumping and take the stairs a bit more slowly. Adding glucosamine and fish oil supplements can help his joints stay lubricated. Check with your vet for guidance on proper dosage.

Doberman Pinschers become seniors at around nine years old.

Beyond helping with arthritis, fish oil and other sources of omega fatty acids also help keep your senior's skin from drying out. Speaking of skin, be sure to maintain the older Dobie's grooming routine. Not only will it feel good to him, but it will allow you to check for any skin changes or unusual growths.

If supplements don't seem to help when your Dobie experiences discomfort, it's time to consult your vet. Prescription pain relievers and anti-inflammatory drugs can make your dog a lot more comfortable. Orthopedic pet beds, ramps, and doggy stairs will also make the older dog more comfortable in his home.

Meanwhile, keep him moving! Arthritis only becomes worse with a sedentary lifestyle, so light to moderate exercise is important. Your Dobie may sleep more as he gets older, but he still needs the physical and mental stimulation of a daily walk or alternative outing with you.

OTHER SENIOR ISSUES

Naturally, your dog's chances of developing serious conditions like cancer and heart disease increase with age, so vigilant health care is crucial. Senior dogs should thus receive semi-annual veterinary checkups. Some dogs develop a form of dementia called canine cognitive dysfunction (CCD), which manifests as confusion, depression, and loss of appetite. Observe your Dobie's demeanor and behavior for any unusual changes.

Urinary incontinence is another issue that some older dogs (and people!) must contend with. They may have to urinate more often or leak urine when relaxed or sleeping. They may even have indoor accidents. There are many possible causes underlying these problems, and a thorough veterinary exam should be conducted to determine what's going on. If reduced organ function is the root cause, special diets or medications can help. Worst-case scenario? Doggy diapers. But it's more realistic to be prepared for more frequent potty trips and washable pet bedding.

Elder care for our pets means catering a little more to their changing bodies, making them as comfortable as possible, and learning from their stoic positivity. The golden years are a bittersweet reminder that our time with them is limited, but there are many wonderful memories yet to be made.

TRAINING YOUR
DOBERMAN PINSCHER

A well-trained dog is a beautiful sight to behold. Who wouldn't admire an impressive dog like the Doberman Pinscher focused on his human and effortlessly executing commands? More importantly, training is part of responsible dog ownership, especially with a breed like the Doberman Pinscher. *You* know your Dobie is running full tilt at that jogger to greet her with wet kisses, but the pepper spray in her hand tells you *she's* not so sure.

The Doberman Pinscher's reputation often precedes him, so his manners must be impeccable if he is ever going to dispel the misconception that the entire breed is capable only of aggression and mutinous behavior. His natural protective instincts, independent nature, and powerful physicality make training a must, not an option.

POSITIVE TRAINING (IS THERE ANY OTHER KIND?)

Dogs want nothing more than to please their humans, so it makes sense to show our pleasure by rewarding them when they do. Enter positive training. Instead of punishing the dog for incorrect behavior, you reward him for desired behavior. This solidifies your dog's trust in you rather than teaching him to fear you, something that results only in making his temperament unpredictable. Forget old-fashioned notions about dominating your dog and establishing yourself as

The Doberman's protective instincts, independent nature, and powerful physicality make training him essential.

the alpha. The days of hitting, jerking leashes, and forcible submission are long gone. Training should be fun, not boot camp. The keys to effective training are positive reinforcement, repetition, and consistency. With these tools, you can train a Doberman to be a delightful companion.

SOCIALIZATION

Socialization is the practice of exposing a dog to all possible

PUPPY POINTER

Socialization should be an ongoing process throughout a dog's life, but the best time to start is between 12 and 20 weeks of age. Don't forget environmental noises when socializing your puppy, sounds we take for granted but that can scare a young dog. Here's a partial list:
- home appliances like washer and dryer, garbage disposal, vacuum cleaner, etc.
- metal bowl dropped on the floor
- television, radio, video games
- car, lawn mower, leaf blower
- ringing telephone, doorbell
- snapping open plastic trash bags
- crumpling paper bags or newspapers

environments and situations that will compose his world. That means learning how to interact with other animals and people of all genders, ages, and races. Well-socialized dogs usually become confident and easygoing, while poorly socialized dogs can become nervous, shy, or fearful. They can also develop bad habits.

HOW TO SOCIALIZE

Early socialization is the best way to help shape your dog's temperament and behavior patterns. This means taking your pup with you as often as you can to as many places as you can. Bring him to places where he's likely to see all types of people. It's a safe bet that few people can pass up an adorable puppy, and the interactions will acquaint him with all types of people.

Walk your Dobie on different types of surfaces and take him for rides in the car. In high-traffic areas where leash walking may be tricky, put him in a wagon or puppy stroller so that he can still see, smell, and hear everything around him. Practice moderation, though—you don't need to take a young puppy to Fourth of July fireworks or a St. Patrick's Day parade.

Use common sense and expose him to as much as possible without overwhelming him. Keep some treats on hand to reward appropriate responses to new people and situations. Above all, lead by example. Dogs pick up on our mannerisms and reactions; your calm, confident demeanor will show your Dobie that there's nothing to fear.

CRATE TRAINING

The crate can be and should be a dog's special safe haven, not a prison. Situations will arise when it's in your dog's best interest to be crated for his own safety and security, and a properly crate-trained dog will happily retreat there. Without crate training, a dog may resist entering the crate, then whine, bark, and generally fuss while he's inside. That's not good for either of you.

A dog's crate should be a comfortable place where he can relax while you are busy or away for a while. It keeps him safely out of trouble when you cannot monitor him. It's also the fast track to potty training because dogs naturally want to avoid soiling their living quarters. And if Great Aunt Betty, who is terrified of dogs, comes to visit, isn't crating your Dobie a nicer alternative than locking him alone in a closed room, only to have him scratch at the door and vocalize?

CRATE SIZE

The proper-size crate is important, especially if you want your Dobie to enjoy spending time in there. A Doberman Pinscher's crate should be large enough

The crate should be your dog's safe haven, not a prison.

for him to comfortably stand up and turn around in while inside. A crate large enough for an adult Dobie will be too large for a puppy, especially during the housetraining process. (A crate that's too big will allow a puppy to potty in one corner and relax in another.)

If you don't want to upsize your crate during your Dobie's growth, start with an adult-size crate and partition off half of it for the puppy. As he grows and needs more room, relocate the partition. Once he's housetrained completely, you won't need the partition at all.

CRATE MATERIAL

Consider a wire crate, which not only provides the maximum amount of ventilation but also allows your Dobie to see what's going on around him so that he doesn't feel sequestered from the rest of the household. Line the bottom of the crate with some newspapers and an old, soft blanket to make it more comfortable.

CRATE LOCATION

Where you put the crate makes a difference in the success of your dog's acclimation to it. Keep the crate in a part of the house where he can still feel like part of the family while enjoying his private retreat. Putting a crate in the garage or in a locked room will only make him feel isolated. Dogs are social animals, and Dobermans, especially, like to be with their humans. Your dog will become comfortable in his crate more quickly if he feels you are near. You can even put your puppy's crate in your room at bedtime, right next to your bed. He'll feel more secure in your proximity, and you'll be able to hear him if he starts to stir or become whiny, a good signal that a potty break might be in order.

HOW TO CRATE TRAIN

It's never too late to crate train, but the earlier, the better. Most breeders introduce puppies to crates by the time they go to their new homes, so you may already have a head start.

1. Begin by leaving the door open to let your Dobie come and go as he pleases. Place a few toys and treats inside to make the idea of going inside enticing. You can even feed your puppy inside the crate at mealtimes to reinforce the idea that the crate is where pleasant things take place.

2. As he grows more comfortable with his crate, try closing the door for a few minutes while you stay nearby. If he starts to whine, resist the urge to open the door or you'll be teaching him that he can get what he wants by whimpering.

Where you put the crate makes a difference in the success of your dog's acclimation to it.

3. Gradually increase the time the door is shut, taking advantage of naps and mealtimes.
4. Work your way up to walking away while the door is shut. Eventually, your Dobie will learn that the closed crate is his own special den where he can be content and still remain a part of the family.

Two caveats: (1) Never crate a dog as punishment. A dog who is put in a crate as a jail cell will never willingly go in and never happily stay in. (2) Never leave your dog (even an adult) crated for more than a few hours at a time—it's simply not fair to confine him for long periods. If you can't leave your dog alone in the house while you're at work, explore other options for his security when you're out of the house.

HOUSETRAINING

When a new puppy comes home, the first order of business is housetraining. Don't expect too much at first, though. Each dog has his own learning curve, and a puppy's young bladder doesn't have much control yet, so patience and persistence are imperative. The general guideline is that a puppy can "hold it" for one hour for every month of his age until he reaches six months, after which time he will have better bladder control. Housetraining requires some commitment because even a dog who learns the concept quickly may not be able to get your attention in time.

STEP 1: CHOOSE A POTTY PLACE

The first step is to teach your Dobie where you want him to potty. But how do you convey that only certain areas are the proper places? Before you bring him home for the first time, collect some urine-soaked litter or mulch from the pup's living area at the breeder's. Scatter it around the outdoor spot you've designated as the latrine. The scent of the litter will tell your pup that this is the right place to go. Take him directly there when you arrive home and wait for nature to take its course. When it does, praise him to the skies.

STEP 2: SET A POTTY SCHEDULE

Puppies typically need to potty after eating, drinking, and sleeping. Take your Dobie out immediately after these events, and patiently wait until he performs. If he doesn't go after 15 minutes, take him back inside and try again in another 15 minutes. Feeding his meals on a regular schedule will help his little body to digest on a schedule, making elimination a little easier to predict. Don't feed close to bedtime, and remove his water dish a few hours before bedtime to improve your chances of a drier night.

Puppies can't hold their bladders all night, so resign yourself to taking your Dobie outside to potty late in the evening and early in the morning. Put some thick newspapers down at one end of his crate for any overnight piddles. If *you* need to get up in the middle of the night to go to the bathroom, take your puppy outside to do the same.

The more consistently you can get him outside to potty, the fewer mixed messages he'll receive about proper elimination sites.

STEP 3: READ YOUR DOBIE'S POTTY SIGNALS

Learning to read your dog's potty signals is an important part of successful housetraining. When he walks around sniffing at the floor, he's

PUPPY POINTER

Housetraining a puppy while you work full time can be a challenge. If you can't get home at lunchtime to take him out, ask a friend or relative to do it, or hire a professional dog sitter to come in a couple of times a day to take the puppy out for potty breaks. Puppies shouldn't be left alone for eight hours, in any event—doing so will only delay housetraining success. More and more businesses are becoming dog-friendly; see if yours will allow you to bring your crated puppy to work with you for a couple of months. Not only will it make frequent potty trips convenient, but it's also great socialization.

indicating that he's seeking out a place to go. If he walks around in a circle, he's probably getting ready to squat. You know what comes next! If you see these signs, say your chosen word to indicate elimination time (like "potty," "outside," or "bathroom"), pick him up, and take him right outside. Don't give him a chance to make a mistake indoors. When he performs outside, praise him heartily and give him a treat.

STEP 4: DEAL WITH ACCIDENTS POSITIVELY

If you catch your pup in the act of soiling inside, don't scold him. He'll think you are angry that he's eliminating at all, not that you disapprove of the location. Immediately remove him to the proper location where he should finish the job. The interruption may be distracting enough that he needs a few extra minutes to get going again. When he does, praise generously to show your approval of *this* potty place.

Indoor accidents are bound to happen when you're not looking, even for the briefest of times. Your reaction will make a difference in your Dobie's progress. Scolding him after the fact won't serve any purpose. Dogs live in the moment, and your pup won't connect your current displeasure with something he did even a few moments ago. Never punish him for your own negligence. Resolve to keep a sharper eye on him, and press onward.

If you catch your pup soiling inside, bring him to the proper location where he should finish the job.

When cleaning up indoor accidents, use an enzymatic cleaner that neutralizes urine and feces odor. These smells can last even after a thorough cleaning, enticing a puppy to eliminate in the same spot, unless they are neutralized. Clean up the accident properly so that your Dobie won't make the mistake again.

STEP 5: HOLD ON TO YOUR PATIENCE

Remember, this trying time won't last forever! By the time he's six to nine months old, a puppy should be pretty well housetrained. If you're adding an adult Dobie to the family, chances are he's already housetrained. Even if he isn't, you're ahead of all the puppy owners in that your adult Doberman Pinscher has a mature physiology. Teaching him where you want him to eliminate and how to let you know shouldn't take that much time.

Dog Tale

Dobermans are so smart that they sometimes discipline themselves, as Austin H. of Severna Park, Maryland, can attest. "Junior will put himself in time-out. If we leave him home alone and he gets into something that we mistakenly left out, when we arrive home he will come outside and sit at attention at the top of the driveway until we tell him that it is okay. You have to see it to believe it."

BASIC COMMANDS

Basic obedience training can begin as soon as your new puppy comes home. Puppies have limited attention spans, so keep these early training sessions short; about ten minutes, tops. Repetition is the key, so expect to go through the motions several times a day. There are five basic commands (often called the "Basic Five") that every dog should learn: *sit*, *stay*, *come*, *down*, and *heel*. These are the ABCs of a dog's education and form the foundation for any advanced training.

SIT

Invariably, the first command a dog learns is the *sit*, and no wonder—he already knows how! The trick is to get him to do it when you ask him to. Begin and end each training session with a *sit* so that even if your Dobie doesn't readily pick up on the next command, you'll inspire confidence by ending on a positive note.

How to Teach *Sit*

1. Stand or kneel in front of your Dobie and show him a treat.
2. Move the treat close to his nose and slowly raise it above his head, still

keeping it in front of him. He will raise his head to follow the treat, and his backside will naturally drop into a *sit* position.

3. Give the *sit* command at exactly the same moment that his head goes up and his rear goes down.
4. Say, "Yes!" to show your pleasure after he sits, and give him the treat and lots of praise.

STAY

The *stay* command could well save your dog's life one day. A dog who obeys the *stay* command won't bolt out an open door, run into the road, or get into other dangerous situations.

How to Teach *Stay*

1. Put your dog into a *sit*.
2. Conceal a treat in your right hand, place it at his nose, and say, "Stay," while making a stop gesture in front of his face with your other hand. Step forward with your right foot to stand in front of him.
3. Let your Dobie sniff and lick the treat in your hand (but not take it) while you count to five, and then step back to your starting position. If he stayed for those five seconds, he's earned the treat. If he stepped out of position when you moved away, start the exercise over.

After your Dobie becomes a pro at the *stay* command, gradually increase the time you ask him to hold the position. Keep in mind that if he isn't holding the extended *stay* and is moving too much, you might be asking him to hold it for too long. This means that it's time for remedial lessons on the basic *stay*. It may take some persistence, but "stay" with it. Practice makes perfect!

COME

Puppies don't need much encouragement to come to their

Puppies don't need much encouragement to join their humans, so the *come* is easily learned.

humans, so this command is easily learned. It gets harder when distractions tempt your Dobie away from obeying you.

Although it's easy to teach, the *come* command can be easily unlearned if it's misapplied. Translation: Never call your Dobie to come to you and then punish him for some other infraction. He won't be able to make the distinction and will think that coming to you reaps punishment instead of reward. You should also beware of overusing the command; your Dobie will be tempted to ignore you if he hears it repeated too often. The goal here is for him to learn to heed your call no matter what else is going on.

How to Teach *Come*

1. Kneel down, hold your arms wide, and say, "Come!"
2. As soon as he starts moving toward you—which will probably be right away—say, "Yes!" or some other encouraging word in a pleased tone. Every step in the right direction is deserving of praise!
3. Praise and treat when your Dobie completes the *come* by arriving in front of you. Later you can put him in a *sit* when he arrives, but for now it's enough that he learns to come to you on command.
4. Once he has mastered the *come* command, move on to graduate school. Introduce distractions like another person or dog to reinforce the message that your *come* command must be obeyed no matter what.

DOWN

This command is a must for all well-mannered dogs. Your Dobie may feel vulnerable in the *down* at first, but it's important for him to master it if he wants to be a true gentleman.

How to Teach *Down*

1. Attach your Dobie's collar and leash and put him in a *sit*, holding the leash in your left hand and a treat in your right.
2. Rest your left hand lightly on his shoulder, moving the treat hand in front of his nose.
3. Say, "D-o-w-w-w-n," in a drawn-out voice, and gradually lower the treat in front of him to the ground. He should follow its path until he's lowered himself to the ground.
4. When he does, heap praise on him and give him the treat.
5. Practice until he's comfortable with the exercise, gradually progressing to saying "Down" in a normal voice.

When he seems to understand the command, you can start working on *down* from a standing position, which is not all that different from the *sit* position.

1. With your dog in a standing position, say, "Down!" and lower the hand with the treat to the floor.
2. He will lower his forelegs into a play bow, at which point you can slowly move the treat on the floor toward his legs. His rear end should naturally go down as you do so.
3. As soon as your Dobie is in the *down* position, give him the treat and lots of praise.

HEEL

"Heeling" means that your dog matches your pace on leash, walking calmly on your left side. It's a useful command for the athletic Doberman Pinscher to learn, or he could end up walking you!

How to Teach *Heel*

1. Put your Dobie in a *sit* next to your left foot with the leash in your left hand.
2. Say, "Heel!" and step off with your left foot. If he doesn't move right away, lightly slap the coiled excess leash against your leg to beckon him.
3. Walk together a few steps, stop, and tell him to sit.
4. Praise him when he sits.
5. Repeat the *heel* exercise. Praise him as long as he stays by your left leg when walking the short number of steps. If he veers off or stops, put him in a *sit* and start the exercise over. Increase the number of steps as he masters the process.

CLICKER TRAINING

Many training methods are employed to train dogs, and one of the most popular is clicker training, a method of positive reinforcement first used by dolphin trainers.

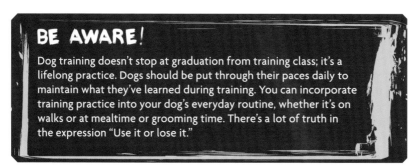

BE AWARE!

Dog training doesn't stop at graduation from training class; it's a lifelong practice. Dogs should be put through their paces daily to maintain what they've learned during training. You can incorporate training practice into your dog's everyday routine, whether it's on walks or at mealtime or grooming time. There's a lot of truth in the expression "Use it or lose it."

Clicker training focuses on fostering a certain behavior, not discouraging it. The clicker makes a recognizable sound used as a signal to mark a desired behavior as soon as it occurs, followed immediately by a reward. The dog quickly learns that the clicker sound means that a reward is imminent and that he can prompt you to make the clicking sound that heralds the reward by repeating the marked behavior.

The advantage to clicker training is that it pinpoints exactly which behavior results in the treat, and it provides a dog with consistent information. Because the clicking noise is different from other environmental cues, it encourages the dog to focus.

FINDING A PROFESSIONAL TRAINER

Most undertakings are made easier with professional guidance, and training your Dobie is no exception. Finding the right training professional is as important as the training itself. She should suit both your and your dog's personality, as well as your philosophy on dog training. A good trainer is fair and consistent. Affection should permeate all aspects of the training.

How do you find such a paragon? Referrals are always best. Ask your vet, your breeder, fellow dog owners, and your local animal shelter. When you've narrowed down the list, observe your top choices at work. Do the dogs in class appear happy and comfortable? Do you like the way the trainer handles the dogs? Talk to some of the students (the human ones, that is). Are they pleased with the results they see in their dogs? Would they recommend this trainer?

If you do the legwork, you should have no trouble finding a responsible, affordable trainer to help you bring out the best in your Doberman Pinscher, and in you!

TRAINING YOUR DOBERMAN PINSCHER

SOLVING PROBLEMS
WITH YOUR DOBERMAN
PINSCHER

Even the most well-behaved dogs have their moments. No matter how well trained your Dobie is, the time will come when he doesn't do "the right thing." Learning to recognize potentially habitual unwanted behaviors is the first step toward correcting them on a permanent basis. "Problem behavior" can be a relative term, but if it's something that annoys or has the potential to harm others, it's a problem that must be corrected.

BARKING

The Doberman Pinscher was developed to be a watchdog, so he instinctively wants to alert you to situations and surroundings. He may be trying to attract your attention because he's not getting enough exercise or attentiveness from you. Generally, it's wise to be aware of what your Dobie is trying to tell you.

But while you don't want to squelch all barking (as important as a Dobie's bark is to his very nature), you have a problem if your Dobie doesn't know when to stop. At the very least, incessant barking will annoy you, your family, and your neighbors. At the worst, it can lead to formal complaints to authorities, drawing negative attention you don't want and the Doberman Pinscher definitely doesn't need.

OBEDIENCE TRAINING

The first step to controlling problem barking is to establish yourself as pack leader through obedience training. This will reassure your Dobie that you can and will handle any situation in which he barks to alert you.

Once your leadership is firmly in place, you can start teaching him the *quiet* command without quelling his protective instincts. When he barks, allow him to alert you to whatever it is, then firmly say, "Quiet!" and distract him from the source, perhaps with a toy. If he stops barking once you've distracted him, praise him and reward with a treat. Remember that he shouldn't be expected to stop

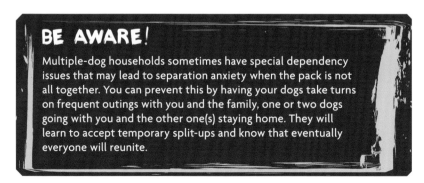

BE AWARE!

Multiple-dog households sometimes have special dependency issues that may lead to separation anxiety when the pack is not all together. You can prevent this by having your dogs take turns on frequent outings with you and the family, one or two dogs going with you and the other one(s) staying home. They will learn to accept temporary split-ups and know that eventually everyone will reunite.

barking if the stimulus increases, such as a stranger approaching the door. Wait until the person has stopped at the door before giving the *quiet* command.

Also remember that a dog left alone or confined for long periods of time may bark out of boredom or anxiety. This shouldn't be considered the same as problem barking. This is a symptom of a different issue that should be handled separately.

SHOCK COLLARS

Bark collars are used to discourage excessive barking by imparting a mild shock, accompanied by a warning buzz, when the dog barks. Because they are often ineffective and can promote aggression, these systems are not recommended for any dogs, especially the Doberman Pinscher.

The Doberman's very origins were as a guardian and protector. He does not typically bark without reason. Beyond the dangers of fostering aggression in your Doberman by shocking him, stifling his barking instinct is attempting to quell the breed's strongest characteristic. Consult a professional trainer if you cannot resolve your Dobie's excessive barking. (Because Dobermans were bred to alert their owners, consider another breed if you worry about loud barking.)

CHEWING

Problem chewing is when your dog habitually chews objects that you don't want him chewing. This is largely an issue for teething puppies. They can and will chew anything they can find. Aside from protecting your belongings, the reason you must manage problem chewing is to ensure your dog's protection. A dog who chews an electrical cord or toxic substance has his safety and health at risk.

REPLACEMENT TRAINING

The best way to prevent unwanted chewing is to provide plenty of safe chew toys to keep your Dobie busy. Chewing is good for maintaining healthy gums and teeth, but be sure the chew toys you provide for your Dobie are especially made for the task. Safe options are appropriately sized and shaped (not small enough to swallow) and sturdy enough that they don't splinter, tear, or break into pieces that can become choking hazards.

If you catch your dog chewing something inappropriate, say "No!" in a firm voice and remove the object (or the puppy from the object). Immediately give him an acceptable chew toy to replace the forbidden fruit. When he starts chewing the proper object, reward him with a "Yes!" and lots of praise. This works especially well with chew toys that contain treats or have flavored coatings.

ADULT PROBLEM CHEWING

Puppies need to chew while teething. While adult dogs also enjoy chewing, an adult Dobie who chews inappropriately is either bored or anxious. Try increasing his mental and physical activity to solve the problem. If that doesn't help, consult a veterinary behaviorist.

DIGGING

While you may consider unwanted digging to be a problem, it actually comes very naturally to your Doberman Pinscher. Dogs dig to root out prey, create a cool resting place in hot weather, or alleviate that devil, boredom.

PREVENTION/DISTRACTION

Problem digging can be challenging to correct, so prevention is your best bet. Don't let your Dobie in the yard or garden unsupervised for long periods of time. Provide plenty of activities when he is out there so that he doesn't resort to digging for lack of something better to do. Keep some toys outside where has ready access to them. You could even hang a tire swing from a tree (the kids will no doubt support this idea).

When chewing problems appear in adults, they often signal deeper issues.

One way to resolve digging is to encourage your dog to dig in certain areas.

ALTERNATIVE DIGGING

If your Dobie has already discovered the joys of digging, close supervision combined with distraction is an option but takes vigilance and consistency. Another option is to *encourage* him to dig, but in a specific place that's just for that purpose. Either fence off a small section or fashion a doggy dirtbox (like a child's sandbox) in a shady area where he can dig to his heart's content without sacrificing your flowerbeds. Bury some toys here to encourage digging in *this* spot. Supervision will be required at first to make sure he doesn't dig in the wrong place, but once he gets the idea of where he's allowed to dig, he'll be happy to get his nose dirty there.

HOUSE SOILING

There is no mystery about puppy accidents. Either you've relaxed your supervision or overestimated your Doberman's bladder/bowel maturity. However, if a housetrained adult Dobie starts soiling indoors, you need to find out why.

First find out if the reason is physical. A urinary tract infection? A parasitic infection? A more serious illness? Have your vet run an analysis of a stool or urine sample. If nothing physical is behind the house soiling, consider when it occurs. If it happens only when you leave the house, separation anxiety could be the reason. It's hard to pinpoint just why this anxious soiling develops in some adult dogs, but if it does, it can be managed:

- Crate your Dobie when he's left alone. He'll instinctively want to avoid soiling the crate, and if he does have an accident, at least your furniture and flooring will be spared. Be careful not to leave him crated for more than an hour or two. If you can't make it back home to let him out, arrange for someone to come over and help.
- Make sure he eliminates just before you leave home, even if he has gone within the past hour. It may take a short leash walk where smells entice him to eliminate, but it's a worthwhile precaution.

House soiling sometimes signals separation anxiety in housetrained dogs.

- Make light of your departure. Too much drama and he'll think there's something to worry about. Put the radio or television on for company (but not too loud) and stuff a toy with a treat or some peanut butter to keep him occupied.
- Neutralize previous accident sites so that residual odors won't tempt him to re-mark the spot.

If all else fails, consider consulting a behavioral specialist for some advice. In extreme cases of incontinence that cannot be controlled, doggy diapers may be the best recourse. Middle-aged females, especially if spayed, often experience age-related incontinence issues that can be treated with prescription medications. Talk to your vet.

JUMPING UP

Dogs jump up on people to greet them at face level. (This may come before or after a good crotch sniff.) This can be endearing in puppies . . . but not so much in a full-grown Doberman Pinscher. Children and the elderly certainly won't enjoy that kind of greeting. Both can be knocked off balance by an enthusiastic Dobie, no matter how friendly his intentions.

PREVENTIVE TRAINING

Jumping up is a behavior that must be corrected as early as possible. The best way to do this is to put your dog in a *sit* before anyone (family or guests) is allowed to pay him any attention. If he's very excitable, tell visitors to completely ignore him until he calms down. The idea is for him to learn that only calm behavior gains him the attention he wants. You can use a leash to reinforce the no-jumping rule until he learns better self-control.

If your Dobie tries to jump on you, turn away and ignore him. When he gives up and stops jumping, turn around and put him in a *sit* before giving him any praise or reward. He'll soon learn that jumping on you doesn't get him the attention he desires. Persistence and consistency are crucial to eliminating this unwanted behavior, but it's well worth the effort. A well-mannered Dobie goes a long way toward dispelling any hype about the breed's "vicious" nature.

NIPPING

Puppies think nipping is fun. They do it to their littermates in a playful manner. While the naturally developing hierarchy within the litter corrects much of their unwanted nipping, we must participate in that hierarchy to let puppies know that humans do not make good chew toys (those needle-sharp puppy teeth *hurt*!). Puppies who nip their humans are treating them as pack equals. This won't do. They must learn to regard humans as pack leaders in order to prevent the nipping from developing into biting.

YELP AND SHUN

You can discourage nipping with the "yelp and shun" method. When your pup nips, give a high-pitched "yelp" (much like a littermate would do to express his displeasure) and turn away, refusing to play with him. He'll learn that nipping

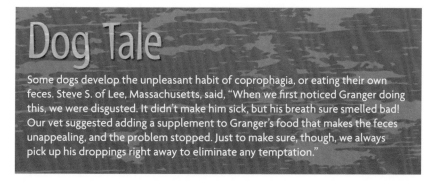

Dog Tale

Some dogs develop the unpleasant habit of coprophagia, or eating their own feces. Steve S. of Lee, Massachusetts, said, "When we first noticed Granger doing this, we were disgusted. It didn't make him sick, but his breath sure smelled bad! Our vet suggested adding a supplement to Granger's food that makes the feces unappealing, and the problem stopped. Just to make sure, though, we always pick up his droppings right away to eliminate any temptation."

only deprives him of the attention he seeks. Redirect nipping behavior by replacing your hand, finger, ear, or whatever with an appropriate chew toy.

WHEN TO SEEK PROFESSIONAL HELP

When is the right time to seek professional help with training? There's no such thing as a wrong time! Even if you're a seasoned dog owner, there's always something new to be learned in a professional training class, whether it's puppy socialization or advanced obedience.

With unwanted behaviors or related issues, an animal behaviorist may be needed. Resources are legion and often just a phone call away. Your veterinarian is usually the first step to obtaining a referral. Your local animal shelter or Doberman rescue organization may also be of help. Doberman breeders are another good source for professional referrals because of their expertise in breed-specific issues.

Animal behavior has become recognized as an important aspect of animal health care, and behaviorist organizations have been established across the world.

Animal behaviorists can help you resolve your dog's problem behaviors.

Notable groups include the International Association of Animal Behavior Consultants (IAABC) (iaabc.org) and the Association of Pet Behaviour Counsellors (APBC) (apbc.org.uk). Both are excellent sources of information and referrals. Dog owners in the United States should also consult the Animal Behavior Society (ABS) (animalbehaviorsociety.org).

What should you look for in a behaviorist? A good behaviorist will ask a lot of questions to discern what kind of help she may be able to provide. She should be well versed in your problem and indicate a commitment to humane training methods. Ask for credentials and references from previous clients. Finding the right behaviorist for you and your dog is paramount for success.

PUPPY POINTER

Aggressive biting, even in puppies, is very different from normal mouthing and play nipping. Should your puppy bare his teeth or snap at anyone, ask your veterinarian for a referral to a dog behaviorist or trainer who specializes in aggression problems. Even if your puppy is exhibiting nothing more than a lot of chutzpah, don't ignore the issue. You need to gain control as quickly as possible. True aggression problems don't work themselves out, so seek professional help as soon as any issues arise.

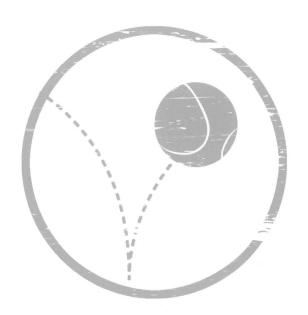

ACTIVITIES WITH YOUR
DOBERMAN PINSCHER

Since Doberman Pinschers are so fast, agile, and generally athletic, it seems a shame to waste all that natural talent merely chasing tennis balls. Not that there's anything wrong with a rousing game of fetch, but who wouldn't get a little bored repeatedly throwing and retrieving a ball? Remember, the Doberman is a working breed who's at his best accomplishing something productive in mind and body. And he'll be at his happiest doing activities with you.

SPORTS AND ACTIVITIES

Dobies love to show off their impressive athletic abilities, making them excellent candidates for a wide variety of sports and activities. You'll be spending quality time together and getting beneficial exercise, too.

AGILITY

Tantamount to a timed obstacle course for dogs, the sport of agility is fast and exciting for both you and your Dobie. This sport requires much skill, and as such, the Doberman Pinscher is well suited to it. The obstacles often resemble those used to train police or military dogs. Jumps, tunnels, seesaws, and A-frames are usually included in the course, all perfect for an energetic Doberman.

Doberman Pinschers
are perfect candidates
for agility.

Competitive agility requires a lot of training and preparation, but there are many resources to help get you started. Most dog-training facilities offer agility classes, and a variety of books on the subject are available at stores and libraries. You can also contact several organizations for information. In the United States, these include the American Kennel Club (AKC), the United Kennel Club (UKC), the North American Dog Agility Council (NADAC), and Canine Performance Events (CPE). In Great Britain, competitive agility is governed by the Kennel Club (KC).

CANINE GOOD CITIZEN® PROGRAM

The Canine Good Citizen (CGC) program was established in 1989 by the AKC as a means of emphasizing responsible dog ownership and the importance of teaching dogs good manners. This program is a wonderful starting point for your Dobie's sporting life because it accomplishes multiple things at once. In addition to training your dog to have impeccable manners and obedience, CGC certification lays an excellent foundation for many of the skills needed in other organized activities. Moreover, it is required of most therapy dogs, and what better way to perform a good deed while simultaneously disproving the belief that Doberman Pinschers are vicious man-eaters?

The CGC test consists of ten sections assessed by an evaluator:

1. Allowing a friendly stranger to approach
2. Sitting calmly to be petted
3. Allowing handling for grooming and physical examination
4. Heeling on a loose lead
5. Walking calmly through a crowded area
6. Sitting, lying down, and staying on command
7. Coming when called
8. Greeting another obedient dog without aggression or excitement
9. Coping with distractions and distracting environments
10. Behaving well in someone else's care while the owner is out of sight

While CGC candidates are performing these tasks, their owners are permitted to praise and encourage them, but inducements like treats and toys are forbidden. Grounds for failure include aggression, elimination or territory marking, whining, and other prominent displays of nervousness.

CONFORMATION

Conformation competition focuses on your dog's physical and temperamental characteristics when compared with the breed standard. Winning dogs most closely adhere to the published breed standard, elevating their value as breeding stock. Conformation is all about the betterment of the breed, and serious breeders want to keep desirable genetic qualities by breeding dogs who closely match the ideal in body and temperament.

If your Dobie is of show quality and you want bragging rights for the beautiful specimen that he is, conformation shows just might be for you. Dog showing requires a good deal of self-education and commitment, though. You'll need to attend local dog shows, study the breed standard, and seek expert advice on what you can expect and what will be expected of you.

Training for the Canine Good Citizen (CGC) test helps you teach your Doberman basic manners and obedience.

OBEDIENCE

So your Dobie graduated at the top of his puppy class, picking up the Basic Five commands as if they were child's play. Why not take his skills to the next level with competitive obedience?

AKC-sponsored obedience trials showcase a handler's training ability and the dog's willingness to perform on command. Competition is divided into different skill levels, which gives newbies a chance to compete while still in the early stages of training. This system also provides motivation to work toward more advanced skill levels.

The Novice level offers the title of Companion Dog (CD) and requires skills such as *come* (recall), staying with a group of dogs, heeling on and off leash, and standing still for examination. Dogs holding the CD title can proceed to the Open level, which leads to the Companion Dog Excellent (CDX) title. Open-level competition requires dogs to perform some skills for longer periods of time and adds additional skills, like retrieving and jumping.

Advancing further, the Utility level awards the title of Utility Dog (UD) and includes directed jumping, directed retrieving, and scent discrimination. Consistent performers who earn the UD title may go on to earn the Utility Dog Excellent (UDX) title. Beyond that stage, dogs may compete for advanced honors like the prestigious Obedience Trial Champion (OTCH) title.

No matter how driven you are, obedience competition is a rewarding way to bond with your Dobie while he achieves a sense of purpose in the tasks you set him to perform. What more could a working dog ask for?

RALLY

An outgrowth of formal obedience, rally (short for "rally obedience") is a newer sport with widespread appeal because of its less strict regimen and more user-friendly environment. Rally actively involves handlers who are encouraged to talk to and praise their dogs as they compete. Having fun is the watchword in rally competition!

Created by dog aficionado Bud Kramer and accepted by the AKC in 2005 as an official event, rally retains the challenge of good obedience performance but loses the somber rigidity of formal obedience competition. Both dog and handler must navigate their way around a numbered course similar to an agility run but with the dog beside his handler in a *heel* position. The numbered stations are usually marked with pylons and symbols indicating which exercise the team should perform at that station. Judges rate the speed and correctness of exercises performed.

Energetic Dobies are well suited to rally, where they will get to perform side by side with their humans. What could be more fun?

PUPPY POINTER

Before adding a Doberman Pinscher to your family, consider whether or not you plan to participate in conformation showing. If you do, you will need to find a puppy who is show quality, not just pet quality. That means he is already exhibiting the qualities of a good show dog: no disqualifying faults, a well-formed body, a good personality.

The breeder will recognize these traits and identify which pups are potential show dogs and which are not. Be prepared to keep your Dobie intact (no spaying or neutering) throughout his conformation career. Show-quality dogs cost more than pet-quality pups, so factor that into your decision to show or not to show.

SCHUTZHUND

The sport of Schutzhund (German for "protection dog") tests a dog's skills in performing the jobs he was bred for: protection, tracking, and obedience. Developed for testing working dogs, Schutzhund has gained greater public interest, especially with owners of breeds like the Doberman Pinscher, the American Pit Bull Terrier, and the German Shepherd Dog. Internationally, Schutzhund has become known as IPO

(Internationale Prüfungs-Ordnung), which has different rules and titles. The AKC recognizes titles from both versions of the sport.

Three main titles are at stake in competitive Schutzhund, with each skill level becoming more advanced. Schutzhund I tests obedience skills (such as on- and off-leash heeling, retrieving on a flat surface, and retrieving over a hurdle) as well as protection skills. Competing dogs, who have to be at least 18 months old to qualify, are also made to follow a track their handler laid 20 minutes beforehand.

After dogs obtain the first title and reach 19 months of age, they can compete in Schutzhund II. The tests here are largely the same as the first level's, but they are more challenging. Schutzhund III is for dogs at least 20 months old with both prior titles. With more difficult tests, like tracking a stranger after 60 minutes have passed, this level requires advanced skills. The holder of the Schutzhund III title is the epitome of the working dog.

The best way to start your participation in Schutzhund is to familiarize yourself with all aspects of the sport. Attend Schutzhund competitions, speak to people involved, and read books on the subject. The German organization Deutscher Verband der Gebrauchshundsportvereine (DVG) sponsors IPO competitions in the United States and Canada as well as in Germany. They have a US-based website at dvg-america.com, which provides information on events and training clubs.

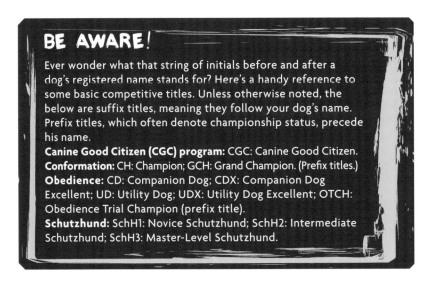

BE AWARE!

Ever wonder what that string of initials before and after a dog's registered name stands for? Here's a handy reference to some basic competitive titles. Unless otherwise noted, the below are suffix titles, meaning they follow your dog's name. Prefix titles, which often denote championship status, precede his name.

Canine Good Citizen (CGC) program: CGC: Canine Good Citizen.
Conformation: CH: Champion; GCH: Grand Champion. (Prefix titles.)
Obedience: CD: Companion Dog; CDX: Companion Dog Excellent; UD: Utility Dog; UDX: Utility Dog Excellent; OTCH: Obedience Trial Champion (prefix title).
Schutzhund: SchH1: Novice Schutzhund; SchH2: Intermediate Schutzhund; SchH3: Master-Level Schutzhund.

SEARCH AND RESCUE

One of the most worthy activities of which your Doberman can partake is search-and-rescue work. Dobies have the strong constitution and adventurous spirit necessary for this work as well as the tenacity and talent for tracking. If you're willing to put in the time and resources necessary, search

Born in January 1975, Bingo von Ellendonk was the first Doberman Pinscher to achieve a perfect score of 300 points in Schutzhund III. He was also credited with improving the working temperament of the Doberman in Europe, passing his hardy disposition on to numerous offspring.

and rescue may be a rewarding job for you and your Dobie.

Search-and-rescue training involves obedience, agility, retrieving, and tracking. It can take a year or more to develop the necessary proficiency, so only the most capable dogs and dedicated handlers should pursue it. Handlers will need to be sufficiently physically fit for the job's demands and have wilderness survival skills, collapsed-building safety training, and knowledge of how to operate as a team with other emergency personnel.

If your feel that you and your Dobie have what it takes to become search-and-rescue volunteers, contact the National Association for Search and Rescue (NASAR) at nasar.org for more information.

THERAPY WORK

Therapy dogs provide comfort and emotional support to the elderly and the sick, often in nursing homes, hospitals, and assisted-living facilities. It's been scientifically proven that petting a dog lowers blood pressure, and therapy dogs have even evoked reactions from dementia and Alzheimer's patients who were otherwise unresponsive.

Perhaps one wouldn't think of Doberman Pinschers when envisioning therapy dogs, but they can be very good candidates. The Doberman's size makes him easily reached from beds and wheelchairs, and his short, sleek coat is a plus when visiting healthcare settings.

This doesn't mean that all Dobies would make good therapy dogs. An even temperament and specialized training are definitely more essential than the right height and short fur. A proper therapy dog must be well socialized, friendly, calm, and obedient. Canine Good Citizen (CGC) training is an excellent starting point for potential therapy dogs.

Therapy work is not just about your Dobie; it requires commitment from you too. Proper and thorough training is vital. So is your willingness to dedicate the time and resources necessary for this worthwhile activity. Patients look forward to regular visits from therapy dogs, and chronic lateness or unreliability will cause disappointment. However, the fulfillment you gain from bringing happiness to others will more than outweigh any inconveniences.

Check with a therapy dog organization to see how you and your Doberman can get involved with this great cause. One of the most prominent organizations is Therapy Dogs International (TDI) (tdi-dog.org), founded in 1976 by registered nurse Elaine Smith, who recognized how beneficial these interactions with dogs could be. The organization continues to certify, insure, and register therapy dogs internationally.

TRAVELING WITH YOUR DOBERMAN PINSCHER

Dogs are social animals who like to be with their humans, Dobermans especially so. Of course, your Dobie can't go with you every time you leave the house, but don't think you can't travel with him. With the right preparations, you can take him on a Sunday drive, a camping trip, or a visit to friends or relatives.

CAR TRAVEL

Your dog's safety in the car is as important as that of any other passenger. A responsible owner makes sure her Dobie is comfortably restrained with a dog safety harness or in a crate that is firmly secured. Aside from the obvious safety benefits in case of accident, a properly restrained Dobie can't suddenly jump up on the driver or otherwise disrupt vehicle control.

If you want your traveling Dobie to ride inside his crate, make sure it's firmly strapped in place (in the case of vans or RVs, bolted down to the vehicle floor.) A crate is only safe for car travel if, during a sudden stop or collision, it can't go flying with your dog inside.

A few hard-and-fast don'ts for car travel:

• Never let your Dobie ride unrestrained in an open truck bed. Not only is it against the law in some areas, but it's plain risky. A sudden stop can send him

Dogs are great for car travel, but they should be properly secured at all times.

tumbling around the truck bed, or worse, out into traffic. If he sees something irresistible, he may jump *out* of the truck bed, even while the vehicle is in motion. In the event of an accident, well—you can only imagine.

- Never let your Dobie hold his head outside the vehicle window, no matter how much you know he enjoys it. Flying debris can seriously injure his eyes and ears.
- Never should you ever leave your Dobie in a parked car, even with the windows open. Even in moderate temperatures, the interior of a car can heat up rapidly like a greenhouse and cause heatstroke. Open windows won't sufficiently ventilate the vehicle to spare your Dobie serious injury or death. If you can't avoid leaving him in a parked car while traveling, don't take him with you.

AIR TRAVEL

There may come an occasion where air travel is your dog's only travel option. Because only service dogs are allowed to ride in an airplane's passenger cabin— (unless your dog is small enough to fit into a crate underneath the seat, and even then, you must reserve his spot ahead of time), a flying Doberman would have to ride crated in the belly of the airplane—and that's a stressful place to be.

Yes, the cargo area is heated when live animals are present, but it's noisy,

Depending on your dog's size, air travel may be more trouble than it's worth.

dark, and lonely down there. It used be common practice for vets to prescribe sedatives to flying dogs, but some experts believe that the decreased heart and respiration rates these medications cause are more dangerous than the emotional stressors themselves.

In recent decades, airlines have responded to these concerns by taking a hard look at the number of dogs who have died during air travel. Conditions have since improved. Animals are no longer left with the luggage on the noisy, hot or cold tarmac; they are loaded last and unloaded first. Another precaution is that, depending on your destination and the season, air travel may not be possible on some airlines due to extreme temperatures. If you want to fly a dog at the peak of summer to Mexico, you may have to rearrange your travel plans.

Still, air travel is not a pleasant prospect for a dog. At best, it's unfamiliar, dark, and loud. Don't forget the real possibility of erroneously checked crates that miss connections or are misloaded (a dog bound for Oakland could end up in Auckland). Moreover, foreign countries may have different quarantine laws to which your dog may be subject, as well as certain vaccination requirements. Even Hawaii has strict quarantine laws, to preserve the state's rabies-free status. If you need to fly your Dobie, do your homework and take every precaution for his comfort and safety.

PET-FRIENDLY LODGING

Pet-friendly accommodations are increasingly easy to find but not so ubiquitous that you shouldn't plan ahead. Even hotels and motels that welcome pets have a limited number of rooms available for them, and those can fill up fast during peak travel periods. Additionally, some hotels that allow pets have restrictions on the size or weight of the dogs they welcome, or they may only accept cats. So it behooves you to contact the hotel or motel directly for all the specifics.

Most pet-friendly lodgings require a small deposit against any damage caused by your pet. Sometimes the deposits are nonrefundable, amounting to an extra fee used to deodorize and thoroughly clean the room for the next guests. This is a justifiable charge, as no one wants to stay in a room with lingering pet odors or stains.

Play by the rules and don't smuggle your dog into a hotel with a no-pets policy (as if you could effectively conceal a Doberman Pinscher). If the staff is unaware that the room needs special cleaning, subsequent guests with allergies could pay the price. Nor should you ever leave your Dobie in the car all night while you sleep in a hotel that doesn't accept pets. Aside from the temperature issue, there's always a risk of theft (despite the Doberman Pinscher's perceived deterrent value).

The Internet is the best place to search out pet-friendly accommodations. Websites such as petswelcome.com, dogfriendly.com, and petscanstay.com showcase a variety of lodgings to suit individual needs. Wherever you go with your dog, remember that you are an ambassador for all guests traveling with pets. Be considerate and treat the lodging as you would your own home. Bring along some poop-clean-up bags, stain remover (just in case), and an old sheet or blanket to throw on the bed or couch. Enjoy your stay and leave the room in as good a condition as—if not better condition than—you found it. Your fellow pet travelers will thank you.

WHEN YOU CAN'T TAKE YOUR DOBERMAN WITH YOU

As much as we would like to take our pets with us whenever and wherever, often that's just not feasible or in their best interest. And unlike cats, who are pretty self-sufficient, dogs who stay home rely on someone being present to provide them with food, water, and interaction.

Yes, there are self-feeding and self-watering contraptions, and you can have someone stop by once or twice a day to let your dog out, but that's a pretty lonely scenario for a dog, especially one who loves his humans as much as the Doberman does. Better to leave him in the responsible care of someone who understands how much your dog means to you.

In-Home Pet Sitters

Pet sitting, especially overnight pet sitting, has become a flourishing business as more people want to leave their dogs in the comfort of their own homes. Not only does your dog get the companionship and care he needs in familiar surroundings, but you get the added bonus of having someone watch your house, take in your mail, and water the plants. Reliable in-home pet care is one of the best ways to keep your dog happy while you're gone and give you peace of mind that he's in good hands.

The only drawback to this type of service is the Doberman's natural tendency to protect his home. The best pet sitter in the world isn't much good if the dog won't let her in the house! When you've hired a pet sitter, have her come over for several brief visits before you leave on your travel. Your Dobie will see that she is welcomed into your home and get to know her a little bit before she actually comes to stay.

Needless to say, you don't want to entrust your home and dog to just anybody. Ask your fellow dog owners, your vet, your breeder . . . anyone you trust in the dog community who might be able to refer you to a reliable, trustworthy pet sitter.

Evaluate your pet sitter carefully, and sufficiently introduce her to your Dobie!

As with any pet-care service, careful evaluation of qualifications should be conducted before hiring anyone. Have potential sitters visit your home to discuss their duties and see how they and your dog take to each other. Find out what kind of experience they have with dogs: Have they ever worked in a veterinarian's office? Have they owned dogs themselves? Do they share your views and feelings about pets? What backup plans do they have in case an emergency prevents them from tending to their canine charges?

Some boarding kennels offer scenic walking trails for their guests.

Additionally, if you haven't received personal referrals, ask if they are insured and bonded. Request some references whom you can consult.

Once you've hired your sitter, introduce her to immediate neighbors that she might call on for help, if needed. This will also prevent your neighbors from wondering if someone is invading your home. Make sure your sitter knows emergency contact numbers and how to get to your veterinarian and emergency clinic.

Boarding Kennels

For a long time, boarding kennels were the only options for extended dog care, and they were usually small indoor kennels with few creature comforts and maybe an outdoor run. Fortunately, contemporary boarding kennels have met the higher standards required by today's dog owners by providing specialized care, comfortable accommodations, and plenty of socialization, exercise, and TLC.

Before you book your Dobie's reservation anywhere, visit several recommended kennels in your area to evaluate their suitability. Are the facilities clean? Does the staff-to-client ratio make sure that every guest receives enough attention? What kind of food do they provide, or do they require clients to provide their own food? Are the grounds well maintained? Do the guests you observe there seem content and well cared for?

Many boarding kennels offer such features as webcams (so pet owners can check in on their beloved companions via the Internet); "luxury suites" that include "sofas" and wall-mounted television sets showing Animal Planet on a continuous basis; playgrounds with specialized dog equipment and toys; and scenic walking trails for extended walks that are more than just an elimination opportunity. These high-end kennels may not be the least expensive around, but many people think their dog's comfort is well worth the price tag.

RESOURCES

ASSOCIATIONS AND ORGANIZATIONS

BREED CLUBS

American Kennel Club (AKC)
8051 Arco Corporate Drive,
Suite 100
Raleigh, NC 27617-3390
Telephone: (919) 233-9767
E-mail: info@akc.org
www.akc.org

Canadian Kennel Club (CKC)
200 Ronson Drive, Suite 400
Etobicoke, Ontario M9W 5Z9
Telephone: (416) 675-5511
Fax: (416) 675-6506
E-mail: information@ckc.ca
www.ckc.ca

Doberman Pinscher Club of America (DPCA)
E-mail: dpcapubliceducation@dpca.org
www.dpca.org

Fédération Cynologique Internationale (FCI)
FCI Office
Place Albert 1er, 13
B-6530 Thuin
Belgique
Telephone: +32 71 59.12.38
Fax: +32 71 59.22.29
www.fci.be

The Kennel Club (UK)
Telephone: 01296 318540
Fax: 020 7518 1058
www.thekennelclub.org.uk

United Kennel Club (UKC)
100 E. Kilgore Road
Kalamazoo, MI 49002-5584
Telephone: (269) 343-9020
Fax: (269) 343-7037
www.ukcdogs.com

PET SITTERS

National Association of Professional Pet Sitters (NAPPS)
1120 Route 73, Suite 200
Mount Laurel, New Jersey 08054
Telephone: (856) 439-0324
Fax: (856) 439-0525
E-mail: napps@petsitters.org
www.petsitters.org

Pet Sitters International (PSI)
Telephone: (336) 983-9222
E-mail: info@petsit.com
www.petsit.com

RESCUE ORGANIZATIONS AND ANIMAL WELFARE GROUPS

American Humane Association
1400 16th Street NW, Suite 360
Washington, DC 20036
Telephone: (800) 227-4645
E-mail: info@americanhumane.org
www.americanhumane.org

American Society for the Prevention of Cruelty to Animals (ASPCA)
424 E. 92nd Street
New York, NY 10128-6804
Telephone: (212) 876-7700
www.aspca.org

Royal Society for the Prevention of Cruelty to Animals (RSPCA)
RSPCA Advice Team
Wilberforce Way
Southwater
Horsham
West Sussex
RH13 9RS
United Kingdom
www.rspca.org.uk

SPORTS

International Agility Link (IAL)
85 Blackwall Road
Chuwar, Queensland
Australia 4306
www.lowchensaustralia.com/shows/international-agility-link.htm

LV DVG America
www.dvg-america.com

North American Dog Agility Council (NADAC)
24605 Dodds Road
Bend, Oregon 97701
www.nadac.com

North American Flyball Association (NAFA)
1333 West Devon Avenue, #512
Chicago, IL 60660
Telephone: (800) 318-6312
Fax: (800) 318-6312
E-mail: flyball@flyball.org
www.flyball.org

United States Dog Agility Association (USDAA)
PO Box 850955
Richardson, TX 75085
Telephone: (972) 487-2200
Fax: (972) 231-9700
www.usdaa.com

World Cynosport Rally
PO Box 850955
Richardson, TX 75085-0955
Telephone: (972) 487-2200
Fax: (972) 231-9700
www.rallydogs.com

THERAPY
Alliance of Therapy Dogs (ATD)
PO Box 20227
Cheyenne, WY 82003
Telephone: (877) 843-7364
Fax: (307) 638-2079
E-mail: therapydogsinc@
qwestoffice.net
www.therapydogs.com

Pet Partners
875 124th Ave NE, #101
Bellevue, WA 98005
Telephone: (425) 679-5500
www.petpartners.org

Therapy Dogs International (TDI)
88 Bartley Road
Flanders, NJ 07836
Telephone: (973) 252-9800
Fax: (973) 252-7171
E-mail: tdi@gti.net
www.tdi-dog.org

TRAINING
American College of Veterinary Behaviorists (ACVB)
College of Veterinary Medicine,
4474 TAMU
Texas A&M University
College Station, Texas 77843-4474
www.dacvb.org

American Kennel Club Canine Health Foundation (CHF)
PO Box 900061
Raleigh, NC 27675
Telephone: (888) 682-9696
Fax: (919) 334-4011
www.akcchf.org

Animal Behavior Society (ABS)
2111 Chestnut Ave, Suite 145
Glenview, IL 60025
Telephone: (312) 893-6585
Fax: (312) 896-5619
E-mail: info@
animalbehaviorsociety.org
www.animalbehaviorsociety.org

Association of Professional Dog Trainers (APDT)
2365 Harrodsburg Road A325
Lexington, KY 40504
Telephone: (800) 738-3647
Fax: (864) 331-0767
apdt.com

Certification Council for Professional Dog Trainers (CCPDT)
Professional Testing Corporation
1350 Broadway, 17th Floor
New York, NY 10018
Telephone: (855) 362-3784
E-mail: administrator@ccpdt.org
www.ccpdt.org

International Association of Animal Behavior Consultants (IAABC)
565 Callery Road
Cranberry Township, PA 16066
iaabc.org

National Association of Dog Obedience Instructors (NADOI)
7910 Picador Drive
Houston, TX 77083-4918
Telephone: (972) 296-1196
E-mail: info@nadoi.org
www.nadoi.org

VETERINARY AND HEALTH RESOURCES
Academy of Veterinary Homeopathy (AVH)
PO Box 232282
Leucadia, CA 92023-2282
Telephone: (866) 652-1590
Fax: (866) 652-1590
theavh.org

American Academy of Veterinary Acupuncture (AAVA)
PO Box 803
Fayetteville, TN 37334
Telephone: (931) 438-0238
Fax: (931) 433-6289
www.aava.org

American Animal Hospital Association (AAHA)
12575 W. Bayaud Ave
Lakewood, CO 80228-2021
Telephone: (303) 986-2800
Fax: (303) 986-1700
E-mail: info@aaha.org
www.aaha.org

American College of Veterinary Internal Medicine (ACVIM)
1997 Wadsworth Boulevard
Lakewood, CO 80214-5293
Telephone: (303) 231-9933
Telephone (US or Canada): (800) 245-9081
Fax: (303) 231-0880
E-mail: acvim@acvim.org
www.acvim.org

American College of Veterinary Ophthalmologists (ACVO)
PO Box 1311
Meridian, ID 83680
Telephone: (208) 466-7624
Fax: (208) 466-7693
E-mail: office15@acvo.org
www.acvo.org

American Heartworm Society (AHS)
PO Box 8266
Wilmington, DE 19803-8266
E-mail: info@heartwormsociety.org
www.heartwormsociety.org

American Holistic Veterinary Medical Association (AHVMA)
33 Kensington Parkway
Abingdon, MD 21009
Telephone: (410) 569-0795
Fax: (410) 569-2346
E-mail: office@ahvma.org
www.ahvma.org

American Veterinary Medical Association (AVMA)
1931 North Meacham Road, Suite 100
Schaumburg, IL 60173-4360
Telephone: (800) 248-2862
Fax: (847) 925-1329
www.avma.org

ASPCA Animal Poison Control
Telephone: (888) 426-4435
www.aspca.org/pet-care/animal-poison-control

British Veterinary Association (BVA)
7 Mansfield Street
London
W1G 9NQ
United Kingdom
Telephone: 020 7636 6541
Fax: 020 7908 6349
E-mail: bvahq@bva.co.uk
www.bva.co.uk

Orthopedic Foundation for Animals (OFA)
2300 E. Nifong Boulevard
Columbia, MO 65201-3806
Telephone: (573) 442-0418
Fax: (573) 875-5073
E-mail: ofa@offa.org
offa.org

US Food and Drug Administration Center for Veterinary Medicine (CVM)
US Food and Drug Administration
Communications Staff (HFV-12)
7519 Standish Place
Rockville, MD 20855
Telephone: (240) 402-7002
E-mail: AskCVM@fda.hhs.gov
www.fda.gov/AnimalVeterinary/

PUBLICATIONS
BOOKS
Biniok, Janice. *The Doberman Pinscher.* Terra-Nova. With consulting veterinary editor Wayne Hunthausen, DVM. Neptune City: TFH Publications, Inc., 2010.

King, Trish. *Parenting Your Dog: Develop Dog-Rearing Skills for a Well-Trained Companion.* Neptune City: TFH Publications, Inc., 2010.

Morgan, Diane. *My Dog Is Driving Me Crazy! Be Smarter Than Your Dog! A Practical Guide to Understanding and Correcting Problem Behaviors.* Neptune City: TFH Publications, Inc., 2014.

Palika, Liz. *Doberman Pinscher. DogLife: Lifelong Care for Your Dog.* Neptune City: TFH Publications, Inc., 2011.

Yin, Sophia. *How to Behave So Your Dog Behaves.* Rev. ed. Neptune City: TFH Publications, Inc., 2010.

MAGAZINES
AKC Family Dog
American Kennel Club
260 Madison Avenue
New York, NY 10016
www.akc.org/pubs/family-dog/

AKC Gazette
American Kennel Club
260 Madison Avenue
New York, NY 10016
www.akc.org/pubs/gazette/

WEBSITES
Nylabone
www.nylabone.com

TFH Publications, Inc.
www.tfh.com

INDEX

PHOTO CREDITS

Africa Studio (Shutterstock.com): 34

Aleksandar Kamasi (Shutterstock.com): 115

Aneta Jungerova (Shutterstock.com): 77

Annette Shaff (Shutterstock.com): 138

ANURAK PONGPATIMET (Shutterstock.com): 33

argo74 (Shutterstock.com): 106

atlon11111 (Shutterstock.com): 8

Best dog photo (Shutterstock.com): 52, 75

Callipso (Shutterstock.com): 116

cynoclub (Shutterstock.com): 49, 118

cynoclub (Shutterstock.com): 55

dashingstock (Shutterstock.com): 78

dezi (Shutterstock.com): 63, 130

Dmitry Kalinovsky (Shutterstock.com): 81, 143

Dmytro Zinkevych (Shutterstock.com): 1, 3

DragoNika (Shutterstock.com): 27, 50

Dymtro Zinkevych (Shutterstock.com): 128, back cover

Eric Isselee (Shutterstock.com): front cover, 11, 60

Fotokostic (Shutterstock.com): 28

gillmar (Shutterstock.com): 105, 129

glebTv (Shutterstock.com): 17

Happy monkey (Shutterstock.com): 61

InBetweentheBlinks (Shutterstock.com): 140

Jana Behr (Shutterstock.com): 92, 94, 102, 111

jocic (Shutterstock..com): 12

L. Nagy (Shutterstock.com): 85

Laengauer (Shutterstock.com): 74

Lucky Business (Shutterstock.com): 68, 82

Makarova Viktoria (Shutterstock.com): 51

MaKo-studio (Shutterstock.com): 21

Marie Dolphin (Shutterstock.com): 24

Marlonneke Willemsen (Shutterstock.com): 131

MaxyM (Shutterstock.com): 125

Michelle D. Milliman (Shutterstock.com): 100

Nenov Brothers Images (Shutterstock.com): 45

Nikolai Tsvetkov (Shutterstock.com): 4, 14, 18, 42, 86, 120

Nitr (Shutterstock.com): 46

OlgaOvcharenko (Shutterstock.com): 40, 54, 66

Pavel Shlykov (Shutterstock.com): 6, 9, 80, 90, 141

Photographee.au (Shutterstock.com): 35

photos2013 (Shutterstock.com): 71

Purino (Shutterstock.com): 31, 38, 110, 112, 114, 136

Richard Chaff (Shutterstock.com): 98, 126

Richard Peterson (Shutterstock.com): 30

Robynrg (Shutterstock.com): 57, 96

Tamara83 (Shutterstock.com): 72

VP Photo Studio (Shutterstock.com): 124

WilleeCole Photography (Shutterstock.com): 58

YAN WEN (Shutterstock.com): 16

DEDICATION

For Jackson and the girls.

ABOUT THE AUTHOR

Cynthia P. Gallagher lives in Annapolis, Maryland. A member of the Dog Writers Association of America (DWAA), she is the author of seven single-breed dog books and two novels under the name Cynthia Polansky. Visit her on the web at cynthiapgallagher.com.

ABOUT ANIMAL PLANET™

Animal Planet™ is the only television network dedicated exclusively to the connection between humans and animals. The network brings people of all ages together by tapping into our fundamental fascination with animals through an array of fresh programming that includes humor, competition, drama, and spectacle from the animal kingdom.

ABOUT *DOGS 101*

The most comprehensive—and most endearing—dog encyclopedia on television, *DOGS 101* spotlights the adorable, the feisty and the unexpected. A wide-ranging rundown of everyone's favorite dog breeds—from the Dalmatian to Xoloitzcuintli —this series surveys a variety of breeds for their behavioral quirks, genetic history, most famous examples and wildest trivia. Learn which dogs are best for urban living and which would be the best fit for your family. Using a mix of animal experts, pop-culture footage and stylized dog photography, *DOGS 101* is an unprecedented look at man's best friend.

At Animal Planet,
we're committed to providing
quality products designed to
help your pets live long,
healthy, and happy lives.